DISCOVER YOUR SPIRITUAL GIFT AND USE IT

RICK YOHN

LIVING STUDIES
Tyndale House Publishers, Inc.
Wheaton, Illinois

*To Dad
who provided the freedom
and encouragement for me to
develop my gifts.*

Unless they are otherwise identified,
Scripture quotations in this book
are from the New American Standard Bible

Library of Congress Catalog Card Number 81-86409
ISBN 8423-0626-9, paper
Copyright © 1974 Tyndale House Publishers, Inc.,
Wheaton, Illinois. All rights reserved.

Printed in the United States of America

94 93 92
12 11

contents

foreword

What more effective way to spiritual impotence could Satan devise than to lead believers into the notion that they are useless? To confuse Christ's own followers on the subject of spiritual gifts is to cripple his cause.

God gives gifts to men, and gifted men to the church. Who are these gifted individuals? A select few? What actually do they do? And what about *me*—where can I fit into the picture?

The reader of *Discover Your Spiritual Gift and Use It* is privileged to sit under the capable ministry of Pastor Rick Yohn—to benefit from his pastoral experience and his extensive firsthand study. Realistic and scriptural answers are offered to a myriad of common questions on the whole subject of service for the Master. The author erects signposts leading to many avenues of service which even the newest, most inexperienced believers in the body may follow.

Certainly the entire area of spiritual gifts needs reexamination in today's churches. "Involvement" is a word much used, often misunderstood. For the one who wants to step out of the long gray line of church members and do something for Jesus Christ, here is substantial and varied encouragement.

This warm, informal book deserves to be read and pondered. It is refreshingly simple and biblical—an invincible combination easy to take. Not everyone will agree with the author's conclusions, but all will benefit greatly from exposure to them.

Tired of playing church? Spend a few hours in the following pages. They could alter your Christian life and ministry.

HOWARD G. HENDRICKS
Professor of Christian Education
Dallas Theological Seminary
Dallas, Texas

you've got what it takes

The world is facing a crisis as never before. Blackouts, brownouts, gas and oil shortages are symptoms of the energy crisis. The life style of the average American could be changed drastically within this decade.

But this energy crisis is mild compared to the energy crisis in the life of man. He is powerless to function at peak efficiency. His home is breaking up. His environment is being polluted. His political world is in constant chaos. His personal life is one of insecurity, confusion and purposelessness. He feels as if someone has pulled the plug. His fire has gone out.

Yet God has made a provision for man to experience as much power and ability as he will ever need to live at top efficiency. Where is that potential? It is within you, if you've experienced a personal relationship with God.

"You have everything when you have Christ" (Colossians 2:10, *The Living Bible*). You are complete in him. Whatever purpose God had in placing you on this earth, you have the capacity to accomplish that task. You're equipped to fulfill your call. You have all of the *potential* you need to serve God effectively. You have God's Word, God's power, God's character, and God's gifts.

WHAT GOD GIVES YOU

1. God has supplied you with *his written Word, the Bible*. This Book is more than a collection of religious thought or a composite of ancient ethics. As you try to apply biblical truth to life, you'll increase your capacity to serve God effectively. The Bible demands response. People were impressed with Jesus because he spoke with authority. When he spoke, he expected men to respond. And now you possess authority for your life in the form of God's written Word.

In recent years we've become a nation of joggers. We are running down streets, through fields, and around tracks in hopes of increasing our lung and heart capacity. Those who exercise consistently will decrease their possibility of heart disease. They'll become more effective in their everyday lives.

Likewise, the Christian who consistently studies the Scriptures will decrease his possibility of "spiritual heart disease." He'll develop keen awareness of Christ's reality. He'll be better equipped to serve God. "All Scripture is inspired by God and profitable for teaching, for reproof, for correction, for training in righteousness; that the man of God may be adequate, equipped for every good work" (2 Timothy 3:16, 17). Merely to possess a Bible or a jogger's manual won't keep you healthy. Rather, you must study and use the book.

2. God has equipped you with *his power*. One late afternoon during a typically cold Winnipeg winter, my wife was in the kitchen preparing supper. Our two boys were playing on the floor and I was attempting to hear the evening news. It was a warm, secure feeling to be inside, protected from the −30° weather; a delicious aroma was coming from the kitchen. Physically and emotionally I was preparing for a relaxed evening with the family. Suddenly the TV went off, and as I got up to fix it, I noticed that the house lights were off. I got a flashlight, went out to the kitchen, and discovered that the electric stove was off.

Suddenly a thought hit me. "Was the furnace still working?" According to the thermometer, the house had already cooled several degrees and the furnace refused to start again. I looked out the front window and saw that the street lights were off. Our neighbors' houses were dark.

It's amazing what thoughts go through your mind at such a time. After I got over my disgust that I wouldn't be eating a warm meal, I started to wonder how we would keep warm in our unheated house when it was –30° outside. During the next few hours we prayed, waited, and looked for any sign that electric power was again available. As we sat in our living room with coats and candles, the TV, stove, and furnace suddenly turned on. Power was restored. There we had been with all the necessary equipment to keep life moving at a comfortable pace, but with no power.

Your power is derived from the Spirit of God, whom you received the day you invited Jesus to become your Savior. Whatever your intellect, finances, experiences, reputation, abilities— without God's power, you are like a powerless kitchen stove or furnace.

Have you experienced power failure in your life? In spite of all your abilities, do you seem powerless to resist temptation and to produce spiritual fruit? Turn to the Holy Spirit. Confess your sin. Ask him to restore power in your life. Then thank him for his power and live expectantly.

3. You are also equipped with *God's character.* The world has plenty of unloving, miserable, anxious, impatient, unkind, evil, unfaithful, vengeful people. The fruit of the Spirit is love, joy, peace, patience, kindness, goodness, faithfulness, gentleness, self-control (Galatians 5:22, 23).

This means you have the necessary ingredients to be Godlike. It means you can show Jesus Christ to your family, friends, business associates, neighbors, and fellow students. What a contrast with what man produces in his own energy!

4. God has also equipped you with *spiritual gifts.* These gifts are essential to completion in Christ. They helped you to function effectively and enable you to mature. They prepare you to be a participator in the work of God rather than an observer.

WHAT ARE SPIRITUAL GIFTS?

Spiritual gifts are *special* abilities that God gives you to accomplish his work. The Bible says, "As each one has received a special gift, employ it in serving one another, as good stewards of the manifold grace of God" (1 Peter 4:10).

Spiritual gifts are neither identical to natural abilities nor are they totally different. There are both similarities and differences.

Observe the similarities between spiritual gifts and talents. Both gifts and talents may have their source in God (1 Corinthians 4:7). Both may be used for selfish or godly purposes. Both may produce good or devastating results (Ephesians 4:15, 16; 1 Corinthians 14:23). Even the quality of the talent and gift may be similar. But there are some very definite differences between the two.

1. *Only Christians* possess spiritual gifts. Only those who possess the Holy Spirit possess the gifts of the Spirit (Romans 8:9, 14, 16, 17; 1 Corinthians 12:7). In direct contrast the Bible refers to the unbeliever as the one who does not have these gifts (1 Corinthians 14:16, 23, 24).

2. A second distinction unfolds in the area of *time.* Natural abilities are those talents which man receives at birth. Man cannot develop what was not given him at birth. However, spiritual gifts are given to man both from birth and after his conversion experience. Jeremiah relates God's dealings with him before he was born. "Before I formed you in the womb I knew you, and before you were born I consecrated you; I have appointed you a prophet to the nations" (Jeremiah 1:5). I believe that both the ministry and the gift of prophecy were Jeremiah's from birth. Likewise a Jerome Hines, a Pat Boone, a Johnny Cash were all given their gifts of music before their new birth. However, today they use these gifts for more than mere entertainment.

Furthermore, the Apostle Paul was a gifted teacher and persuader before his conversion (Galatians 1:15, 16; Philippians 3:5, 6; Acts 22:3–5). But his gifts of miracles, healings, tongues, and apostleship were not given to him until after his conversion. Talents come with the natural birth. Spiritual gifts may come from the natural birth (for the potential Christian) and from the second birth, the spiritual birth (John 3:3–8).

3. A third distinction between natural talents and spiritual gifts is *the role with which the Holy Spirit involves himself.* The natural man (1 Corinthians 2:14) is dependent upon himself to discover, develop and use his talent. But the Christian can call on

the Holy Spirit to reveal what gifts he possesses, to discipline him in developing those gifts (2 Timothy 1:7), and to empower him in using those gifts (1 Corinthians 2:4, 5; Philippians 4:13).

In summary, the only positive way to distinguish between a gift and a talent is to determine whether or not the individual possessing the ability is truly born again. If he knows the Lord personally as Savior, his ability may be a spiritual gift. If he is not a Christian, that ability is a natural talent. This will be revealed to him, and often to other Christians, by the Holy Spirit.

A word of caution is in order. Every spiritual gift supplied by the Holy Spirit can be counterfeited by Satan and may be used to influence both Christians and non-Christians.

The magicians of Pharaoh's court had the ability to perform miracles (Exodus 7:11, 22; 8:7). The false prophet in the Tribulation will perform miracles (Revelation 13:13, 14). It is common knowledge that within the various religions of the world the worshippers both heal and are healed, speak in tongues, and perform miraculous feats. As in the days of the apostles (1 John 4:1) so now there are men and women using "prophetic gifts" that get an attentive hearing, but are to be avoided (Deuteronomy 18:22). And who can deny the persuasive ability of Lenin, Hitler, and Castro? They exhort. They preach another gospel. And millions are converted to their philosophy of life.

But where sin abounds, grace much more abounds. And where there is deception and counterfeiting by our great enemy, so are there bountiful spiritual gifts.

These gifts are the possession of every believer, and we are accountable to use them in a way that glorifies God. Jesus said, "Let your light shine before men in such a way that they may see your good works, and glorify your Father who is in heaven" (Matthew 5:16).

Are you producing good works, thereby glorifying God? Many believers aren't, in spite of their tremendous potential.

PROBLEMS THAT LIMIT GOOD WORKS

1. Many Christians face *the problem of unknown potential.* Both philosophy and science agree that most men and women use

less than 30% of their potential. (In fact, an examination after death would reveal millions of undeveloped brain cells.) As the average person is unaware of his or her potential, so the majority of Christians are ignorant of the potential they have in spiritual gifts. Some who recognize their gifts don't know what to do with them.

2. A second problem Christians have is *comparing* themselves with one another. When we do this, we often distort our self-image. We see ourselves as inferior. In his book *Psycho-Cybernetics,* Dr. Maxwell Maltz states, "At least 95 percent of the people have their lives blighted to some extent by feelings of inferiority, and to millions this is a serious handicap to success and happiness."[1]

You don't have to look far to see the results of these attitudes. The needs in the church today are critical, but where are the men and women to meet them? I don't believe that the sole reason for noninvolvement is lack of commitment. Many Christians are convinced they have nothing to offer.

Why do we come to such conclusions about ourselves? Dr. Maltz puts his finger on the problem. "It's not *knowledge* of actual inferiority in skill or knowledge that gives us an inferiority complex and interferes with our living. It's the *feeling* of inferiority that does this.

"And this feeling of inferiority comes about for just one reason: we judge ourselves, and measure ourselves, not against our own 'norm' or 'par' but against some other individual's 'norm.' When we do this, we always, without exception, come out second best. But because we think and believe and assure that we should measure up to some other person's 'norm,' we feel miserable, and second-rate, and conclude that something is wrong with us" (p. 52).

Centuries ago the Scriptures declared: "What stupidity! . . . Our goal is to measure up to God's plan for us" (2 Corinthians 10:12, 13, TLB).

Estimate yourself according to the equipment God has given

---

1 Maxwell Maltz, *Psycho-Cybernetics* (New York: Pocket Books, Inc., 1970).

you. In Romans 12:3 Paul refers to our standard of comparison as the *faith* God has given us. "As God's messenger I give each of you God's warning: Be honest in your estimate of yourselves, measuring your value by how much faith God has given you" (Romans 12:3, TLB). Then, as Paul describes the faith we have been given, he elaborates on spiritual gifts. "God has given each of us the ability to do certain things well. So if God has given you the ability to prophesy, then prophesy whenever you can—as often as your faith is strong enough to receive a message from God. If your gift is that of serving others, serve them well. If you are a teacher, do a good job of teaching" (Romans 12:6, 7, TLB).

This is your yardstick. If you want to develop an accurate opinion of yourself, you must discover the gifts with which God has equipped you and recognize that he has also given you the faith to use them. Your responsibility, then, is to begin to act on this knowledge.

3. A third problem Christians face is *competition.* We have been conditioned since birth to compete with one another. We compete with brothers and sisters for Mother and Dad's attention. We compete with friends for scholastic honors, athletic prowess, and social status. We compete in business for positions and salaries. We compete with our neighbors in accumulating gadgets. We even compete in church.

How do you feel when your best friend is praised for her solo voice? How do you react when your buddy receives acclaim for his scholastic or athletic ability? How do you relate to those who are excellent teachers, efficient leaders, fantastic musicians, popular workers, or skillful in making money? Do you envy them or do you thank God for them? Do you murmur against them or do you encourage them? Do you criticize or compliment them? Your answers to these questions will show whether you have a competitive attitude.

Ignorance of our gifts and an attitude of comparison or competition are problems with which we must reckon. And you can deal with these problems because you've got what it takes: God's Word, God's power, God's character, and God's gifts.

try lending a hand

We are living in the day of the professional and the specialist. With the exception of a few, the family physician is becoming ancient history. Even the neighborhood mechanic is disappearing from everyday life; today we take our cars to the Diagnostic Center.

The church reflects society's trends. Most Christians are willing to turn the "ministry" over to professionals (pastors) and specialists (directors of Christian education, youth directors, ministers of music).

The result is about 20 percent efficiency! The majority of Christians do nothing but attend. But God hasn't designed his church to function at low efficiency: his plan includes the total Body. God wants the complete mobilization of his people. And although you may not be a professional minister, a specialist in Christian service, you're just as useful to him. He may have given you one of those priceless gifts that can be used to lend a hand to others: serving, giving, showing mercy, craftsmanship, or healing.

THE GIFT OF SERVING OR HELPING

Mr. Frank was in his early 60s and full of energy. He impressed me with his friendliness and availability, so I went to him about

9

taking a position on the church board. He had experience and I believed he would be an asset to our board. But Mr. Frank felt his strong point was in helping others. He said, "Pastor, if you want me to provide transportation for Sunday school children, I'll do it. If you want me to pick up a shut-in and bring him to church, I'd be glad to do that. If you want me to visit, I'll visit. If you need help in handing out brochures or circulars, I'm available. I can't teach or sing, but I can help. And that's what I'm offering to do."

My surprised expression caused him to smile, and he added, "I've spent many years on church boards and I've even chaired a few. But I've come to the conclusion that my place is helping people whenever they need help." And that's exactly what he did. Whenever anyone needed help, Mr. Frank was there. He picked up children in his car for Sunday school. He handed out brochures in the community. He took time from his business to help men find jobs.

Perhaps you can identify with Mr. Frank. Perhaps you too have the gift that Paul called *serving.* "And since we have gifts that differ according to the grace given to us, let each exercise them accordingly. . . . if service, in his serving . . ." (Romans 12:6a, 7b). In his letter to the Corinthians the Apostle referred to this gift as the gift of *helps.* "And God has appointed the church . . . gifts of helps" (1 Corinthians 12:28).

This gift refers to the ability to give assistance or aid in any way that brings strength or encouragement to others. There is, however, an attitude that goes along with the gift, which distinguishes helpers who don't possess the gift from those who do.

In most churches the responsibility for preparing food for church banquets is delegated to the women's organization. Some women prepare food because it's expected. Others perform the same task because they enjoy it. I met a woman several years ago who told me that she and her husband cater at various churches because it's the one task they can do as a ministry. She was an excellent cook and her enthusiasm and Christian radiance equalled her ability to cook for church banquets. Whereas many women cook out of responsibility, this woman cooked out of a sense of ministry. She demonstrated the gift of service.

I recently met a gentleman whom I've come to admire, a man

who served God with great commitment but with little public recognition. I have seen him many times working at the church, fixing, planting, and improving the grounds. He wasn't the custodian. He wasn't being paid for his work. But he was serving the Lord with his gift of helps, and his attitude was one of doing it for God—and enjoying it. This was his ministry. Whatever his hand found to do, he did it enthusiastically.

I've seen women work in church nurseries who "put up with" distractions, noise, and dirty diapers. I've also seen the work of Mrs. Field, also a nursery volunteer. She put hours into it. To her, the nursery wasn't a mere Sunday babysitting service, it was a place to minister the love of God to children. She regularly cleaned the toys and mattresses. She made certain her staff was well informed about their responsibility. They knew they could rely on her for help.

Or perhaps you will identify with Jane, who used her gift of helps in the church office. No one paid her to help, but she volunteered to set aside one day each week to run the mimeograph machine. Once the material was printed, she would fold, staple, and mail it.

When I was ministering in Minneapolis, one of our members was a photographer. Though he also served on the church board, his greatest contribution was to be available to use his camera. He shot pictures of social events, returned missionaries, and special occasions. He contributed his time and money to serve as he could. Today he uses his gift of helps to produce church bulletin pictures.

Several years later I came across another photographer in Fresno. He constantly uses his hobby of photography with the gift of serving. At youth outings and parties, adult socials, baby dedications, and graduations, he arrives with camera in hand. The time and expense are his, and he gives pictures to those he thinks will appreciate them.

Another couple I knew set aside every Saturday to go to their church and work on the bulletins. They mimeographed them and placed them in the foyer for the morning worship service.

The Bible provides insight into a man gifted with ability to assist in a way that brought strength and encouragement to another. His name was Onesiphorus. Paul writes of this helper: "May the Lord bless Onesiphorus and all his family, because he visited me and encouraged me often. His visit revived me like a breath of fresh air, and he was never ashamed of my being in jail. In fact, when he came to Rome he searched everywhere trying to find me, and finally did. May the Lord give him a special blessing at the day of Christ's return. And you know how much he helped me at Ephesus" (2 Timothy 1:16, 17, TLB).

Do you realize why Onesiphorus is being praised? Not because he was an intellectual. Not for his position in the church. Not for how many committees he chaired. He was praised for his willingness to visit Paul in prison. He wasn't ashamed to identify with this prisoner. He wasn't so concerned about his reputation that he neglected his responsibility to Paul. He took the guards' suspicious stares and the neighbors' gossip as part of the price to pay for using his gift.

His attitude was tremendous. He could easily have copped out after making several half-hearted attempts to find Paul. Rome was full of prisons, and Onesiphorus had to go from one to another asking, "Do you have a prisoner here named Paul? He is from the city of Tarsus. He is a Christian." Certainly Onesiphorus got tired of looking for Paul. He probably asked himself if it was worth the effort and ridicule. But he continued his search.

When he found Paul, he brought news about how God was working in the lives of others. He may have brought food. He may have spent time praying with him. But whatever he did during those visits, Paul says that Onesiphorus encouraged and refreshed him.

You, too, may have this gift. Your presence with someone who's sick, imprisoned, or shut in can make a great difference in his attitude toward himself, toward God, and toward others. Ability to sit and listen with interest is as important as the ability to speak.

Other opportunities to serve include being on welcome committees, ushering, decorating, planning socials, helping in youth work, and providing and arranging flowers for the sanctuary.

The gift of helps is a gift for which many believers will be rewarded at the judgment seat of Christ. Paul writes, "May the

Lord give him [Onesiphorus] a special blessing at the day of Christ's return'' (2 Timothy 1:18a, TLB).

A reward for visiting and encouraging others? That's exactly what the Scriptures mean. If God has given you the gift of helps or service, he doesn't hold you accountable to preach or to teach. He holds you accountable for giving assistance in any way that brings strength and encouragement to others.

age is no barrier

The Scripture makes no distinction about age when it comes to the distribution of gifts. I knew a young boy still in grade school who wanted to be used by God. When the pastor asked him what he was interested in doing, the boy replied, ''I'd like to help in the children's library.'' Because of his interest and ability, he soon was promoted from assisting in the children's library to managing it. He served the Lord by encouraging children to read books. After both Sunday school and church he would help the children sign out books. He sent cards to the delinquents. He made posters to encourage children to read. He even went into various Sunday school classes and gave a five-minute presentation. Then when class was dismissed he stood outside the classroom with his ''portable'' library, checking out books to borrowers.

''helps'' and evangelism

But is this gift to be used in the church alone? What about using it outside the church? We often think of evangelism as a preaching-centered concept: Get your neighbors into the church and let the preacher get through to them. But have you considered using your gift of helps as an evangelistic tool?

The parable of the good Samaritan (Luke 10:33–37) was given to answer the question, Who is my neighbor? The parable shows that your neighbor is anyone who has a need you can meet. Our neighbor isn't only a man with a spiritual need, whom we try to encourage, coerce, or trick into coming to church with us—that is, if we haven't already written him off as a hopeless heathen. But it's possible he isn't interested in our church or our Lord because we've never demonstrated genuine interest in him as a human being.

Use your gift of helps some day by shoveling the snow from his driveway. Use your gift by cutting his lawn when he's on vacation. Use your gift of service by entertaining your neighbor's children for an afternoon so she can go shopping or just relax. Use your gift to help your neighbor build that garage or addition to his house. Use your gift of helps by being a neighbor who cares.

Other uses of the gift of helps outside the church might include coaching or helping with Little League baseball, midget football, etc. It might include volunteer work at the local hospital, or involvement in a community club. It might include taking time from your job to help a friend find employment. It might mean driving an elderly neighbor to her doctor. " 'Lord, when did we see you hungry, and feed you, or thirsty, and give you drink? And when did we see you a stranger, and invite you in, or naked, and clothe you? And when did we see you sick, or in prison, and come to you?' And the King will answer and say to them, 'Truly I say to you, to the extent that you did it to one of these brothers of mine, even the least of them, you did it to me' " (Matthew 25:37–40).

Jesus Christ honors those who feed the hungry, show hospitality to strangers, clothe the naked, and visit the sick and imprisoned. These are manifestations of the gift of helps. People need help. The Lord's work needs help. And if you can identify with any of the people mentioned in this section, you are one to help.

THE GIFT OF GIVING

Another gift of the Spirit is called giving. "He who gives, with liberality" (Romans 12:8). The gift of service may be the most universally dispensed gift, though it is not necessarily possessed by every believer. The gift of giving is perhaps more limited.

The implication of Scripture is that giving is the ability to make and distribute money to further the cause of God. This gift isn't limited to the wealthy (the "super-rich") in the Body of Christ, but is probably found among many of those whom God has blessed financially. The Apostle Paul writes in particular to those with this gift when he instructs young Timothy, "Tell those who are rich not to be proud and not to trust in their money, which will soon be gone, but their pride and trust should be in the living God who always richly gives us all we need for our enjoyment. Tell them to use their money to do good. They should be rich in good works and should give happily to those in need, always being ready to share with others whatever God has given them. By doing this they will be storing up real treasures for themselves in heaven— it is the only safe investment for eternity! And they will be living a fruitful Christian life down here as well" (1 Timothy 6:17–19, TLB).

Certainly every Christian is responsible to give to the Lord's work. "On every Lord's Day each of you should put aside something from what you have earned during the week, and use it for this offering. The amount depends on how much the Lord has helped you earn" (1 Corinthians 16:2, TLB). "Much is required from those to whom much is given" (Luke 12:48). It has been reported that R. G. LeTourneau made it a practice to give 90 percent of his income to the Lord's work. His attitude toward money is expressed in his autobiography, *Mover of Men and Mountains.* Nels E. Stjenstrom, assistant to the president of Le-Tourneau College, writes in the epilogue, "He does not view money as something to be accumulated for the satisfaction of looking at it, counting each day to check its increase, nor as a measure of man's worth. He sees it only as a means to produce the machine his mind has conceived or as a means to bring men to God . . . Although he has made and spent millions, he is remarkedly detached from money as such; he is only concerned about what it can accomplish. He often says, 'The question is not how much of my money I give to God, but rather how much of God's money I keep for myself.' "[1]

Recently I spoke to a man who has the gift of giving. He told me he knows God has blessed him financially and so he continually looks for needs to which he can give. He said, "Very few

1 R. G. LeTourneau, *Mover of Men and Mountains* (Chicago: Moody Press, 1967), pp. 279, 280.

things give me as much pleasure as giving to the Lord's work." And he has demonstrated his gift by giving to Christian student works, Christian camps, and his local church.

When Paul speaks of the gift of giving he adds a phrase about attitude, "He who gives, *with liberality*" (Romans 12:8). This means we should give with singleness of heart. We shouldn't demand that our name be placed on church furniture. We shouldn't attempt to control the church because of our financial position. We must recognize that money is a gift of God to be used to serve him.

When Paul appealed to those with this gift at Corinth he used the Macedonian churches as an example of proper attitude in giving. "Though they have been going through much trouble and hard times, they have mixed their wonderful joy with their deep poverty, and the result has been an overflow of giving to others. They gave not only what they could afford, but far more; and I can testify that they did it because they wanted to, and not because of nagging on my part. They begged us to take the money so they could share in the joy of helping the Christians in Jerusalem. Best of all, they went beyond our highest hopes, for their first action was to dedicate themselves to the Lord and to us, for whatever directions God might give to them through us" (2 Corinthians 8:2–5, TLB). Then Paul asked the Corinthians to follow suit. "You people there are leaders in so many ways—you have so much faith [the gift of faith], so many good preachers [the gift of prophecy], so much learning [the gift of knowledge], so much enthusiasm [the gift of exhortation], so much love for us [the gifts of helps, showing mercy, etc.]. Now I want you to be leaders also in the spirit of cheerful giving [the gift of giving]" (2 Corinthians 8:7, TLB).

Perhaps God is awakening your conscience to give with liberality. If you are discovering that God is blessing you financially, consider your responsibility. You may not be able to teach. You may not enjoy visitation. You may not have musical ability. But if God has opened opportunities for you to make money, give to his work. Learn the joy of giving.

THE GIFT OF SHOWING MERCY

"What the world needs now is love, sweet love. It's the only thing there is far too little of." No one would argue with that.

The Scriptures declare that the latter days will be filled with violence and brutality (2 Timothy 3:1–4). That's why a person gifted with "showing mercy" sparkles like a diamond against a dark background of indifference. This gift could be described as the ability to work joyfully with those whom the majority ignores: the deformed, crippled, retarded, sick, aged, mentally ill.

I received a letter recently from an elderly lady who quite unconsciously described her gift of showing mercy. She wrote, "I love people and have many sick friends. I visit them and tell them that what God has done for me he can do for them." Here is a 77-year-old using her gift of showing mercy to witness about her faith in Christ. Her sick friends can't argue that she doesn't understand what it's like to be lonely; she lives by herself. They can't argue that she doesn't understand their pain; she's had operations and hospital stays herself. But rather than share her aches, pains, and scars with her sick friends, she demonstrates the love of Christ to them. "When I'm alone and feel that no one cares, I read the Bible and he tells me, 'Even to your old age, I shall be the same, and even to your graying years I shall bear you!' " (Isaiah 46:4a).

Do you enjoy visiting in hospitals, senior citizen homes, jails, or psychiatric wards? If so, thank God for that precious gift and use it for him. But it isn't limited to visiting institutions.

Some married couples demonstrate this gift when they share their homes with friends or in-laws. When elderly parents find themselves alone and old, their children often place them in an institution. I'm not judging those who believe before God that this is best for the parent. In many cases it can be. But happy should be the person whose son or daughter, with the agreement of the spouse, opens his home and welcomes the parent.

Another way this gift manifests itself is when a Christian volunteers to drive an elderly neighbor to the doctor, or grocery store, or takes him out to a restaurant or for a drive. Imagine how older people feel if asked to go for a ride. They're often shut up all day. They may have few or no visitors. They remember the good old days when their legs carried them wherever they wanted to go. Now they're trapped in an old body. Desires and memory are still there, but ability is gone. Can you empathize with the older men and women all around you? Perhaps you possess this gift of showing mercy. You can visit, care, and try to understand them.

A friend of mine has demonstrated this gift since he was a child. His mother told me that many times he would come home with a friend he'd invited for dinner. His compassion for others continued in adult life. A few years ago a foreign student was looking for a place to stay for several days. There was no question whom I could contact. My friend opened his home without hesitation. On another occasion he helped a man who had trouble with alcohol and the law. He gave him money, a job, and encouraged him to come to church.

The Sunday morning that I preached on this gift in my church I closed the service and went to the back of the church to greet people. Coming through the line was a young girl who introduced me to two of her friends. They told me they appreciated this particular message because they were reaping the benefits of the gift of showing mercy. You see, both of these girls were blind. No one else cared enough to bring them to church, but here was a friend who did care and who demonstrated her gift.

Another girl working with Campus Crusade for Christ is using her gift of showing mercy in a similar way. Every week she brings a young man in a wheelchair who has been paralyzed from an automobile accident. When she first brought him he wasn't a Christian, but now he has accepted Christ.

Opportunities to use this gift are unlimited. Innumerable people need it. They have been exposed to nurses, doctors, and volunteers who complain, gripe, dislike each other, and merely put up with their patients. They've had parents who never visit. Some have children who forget they're alive. They've yet to see someone who will love them and care for them *with cheerfulness.* "And since we have gifts that differ according to the grace given to us, let each exercise them accordingly . . . he who shows mercy, with cheerfulness" (Romans 12:6, 8).

THE GIFT OF CRAFTSMANSHIP

An interesting Old Testament passage describes one of the gifts not mentioned in the New Testament. Perhaps the New Testament doesn't list it because the emphasis of the early church was to build men rather than buildings.

But when God told Moses to build the tabernacle he asked him to contact a man named Bezalel. And then he described him to Moses. "I have filled him with the Spirit of God in wisdom, in understanding, in knowledge, and in *all kinds of craftsmanship*" (Exodus 31:3). Notice that these gifts came from the Holy Spirit. They were spiritual gifts, and "craftsmanship" was included.

God went on, ". . . To make artistic designs for work in gold, in silver, and in bronze" (Exodus 31:4). A man who uses such a gift today would be called a silversmith, goldsmith, or coppersmith. He is an artist who expresses his gift by working in metal.

A second way to use this gift is expressed in the next verse. "And in cutting of stones for settings" (Exodus 31:5a). Today we call these gifted men stonemasons. I know a man who has made his entire living carving stones into cemetery monuments. And if you don't think it takes a gift to design and carve gravestones, you have only to begin chiseling at a piece of stone and watch the destruction of a beautiful rock.

Others who work with stones are jewelers. Only skillful hands can guarantee success in cutting a valuable diamond, ruby, or other precious stone.

God continues to explain that this gift is to be used in still another way: "And in the carving of wood" (Exodus 31:5). This brings to mind the carpenter and cabinetmaker as well.

A fourth way to use the gift of craftsmanship is given in the tenth verse, where woven garments were to be designed and produced by Bezalel's helpers. Tailors and dressmakers. And further, ". . . to make *artistic designs*. . . ." (Exodus 31:4). The designer, interior decorator, engineer, draftsman, and artist.

But can we call this a spiritual gift? Perhaps Bezalel and those other men just inherited these natural abilities from their parents. Notice the passage carefully. "And I have filled him with the Spirit of God . . . in all kinds of craftsmanship . . . and in the hearts of all who are skillful I have put skill, that they may make all that I have commanded you . . . the tent . . . the ark . . . the mercy seat . . . all the furniture . . . the table . . . its utensils . . . the pure gold lampstand . . . the altar of incense . . . the altar of burnt offering . . . the laver . . . the woven garments . . . the anointing oil . . . the fragrant incense. . . ." (Exodus 31:3, 6–11).

You see, God is the One who gives the gift of craftsmanship to men. Man may not acknowledge this gift from God, he may never use it for God, but it is a gift nevertheless.

craftsmanship and the church

Can this gift be used for God in the church today? Certainly. Many local churches are blessed with those gifted with craftsmanship. Men use it to build church buildings, to make church furniture, to remodel, beautify, and maintain the property.

One woman used her craftsmanship to decorate the new nursery, and it became a highlight of the building because of her touches. An older man in the same church used his gift to make blackboards and cabinets for the Christian education building. He also painted and printed signs for the front of the church.

craftsmanship and the world

But craftsmanship doesn't have to be limited to the church building. If this is your gift, use it to develop relationships between yourself and your neighbor. Maybe he could use your mechanical ingenuity when his car won't start or when his engine needs a tune-up. Maybe his lawnmower is broken. You don't need the gift of evangelism to witness for Jesus Christ. You can open the door with the gift of craftsmanship.

If you have sewing ability, have you considered making clothes for a neighbor or friend who has more children than she can afford to clothe? Or what about giving a neighbor something you've made with your hands, as a gesture of friendship? It may open doors for you eventually to tell her what Jesus Christ has done for you.

It's a shame when Christians walk around with inferiority feelings and think, "I'm just a mechanic." "I'm just a carpenter." "I'm just a housewife." "God can never use me. I'm not gifted like other people."

Nonsense. You *are* gifted. And if your gift is craftsmanship it's essential for your spiritual welfare that you discover, develop, and use this gift to make disciples for Jesus. If you don't use your gift, you experience frustration and defeat in life. You forever wonder why God has put you on earth.

Don't try to be what you're not. Develop what you have, and become what God wants you to be. Watch him open doors for you.

Now let's take a look at another important manifestation of the gift of helps—that of the healing ministry.

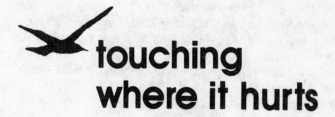

touching
where it hurts

Stanley Powell's legs were injured in an automobile accident six years ago. He has gone to every specialist in the city, but his legs remain paralyzed.

Several Sundays ago, Stan was watching a religious service on television. He saw people standing in a healing line. Then he noticed a man in a wheelchair. The faith healer placed his hands on the invalid. As the camera zoomed in on the man's face, tears filled his eyes. The expression of despair suddenly changed to a broad smile:

"I can feel it! The power! It's coming into my legs." The invalid got up from his wheelchair. He jumped. He stamped his feet. He ran from the platform shouting, "Hallelujah! Praise Jesus!"

Stan was understandably impressed. He loved the Lord. But he had resigned himself to thinking his accident was part of God's will for him. As the TV program closed, Stan noticed that it originated from his own city.

The following Sunday he persuaded a neighbor to take him to the service. The preacher asked for those who wanted healing to come forward. Stan's neighbor wheeled him to the platform. Excitement, fear, and a sense of expectancy gripped his heart. He pictured himself leaving his wheelchair and jumping up and down.

The preacher's hands were warm. Stan looked into the eyes of the faith healer. They were compassionate. Now Stan's hopes were lifted even higher. The preacher spoke. His words filled the tent. "In the name of Jesus of Nazareth, be healed!"

Stan waited. Oh, how he wanted to feel that power surge through his legs. "Do you feel anything?" the preacher asked. "Not yet, sir," replied the puzzled invalid. "Oh Lord, give this man the use of his legs. Let your power permeate his body. Heal him! In the name of Jesus, heal him!"

The atmosphere was tense in the silent auditorium. "How about it? Can you move your toes?" "No," said Stan. "I'm trying. I'm really trying. Oh God, heal me! I'm trying. But it isn't working. My legs are still dead."

"I'm sorry, Mr. Powell. You'll have to leave the platform. Perhaps we can try again later." The preacher motioned Stan off the walkway. "Next, please."

Brokenhearted, confused, Stan went back to his home. He still watches that TV program every Sunday morning. But every time a handicapped person is given use of his legs or arms, Stan silently questions, "Why not me, Lord? What did I do wrong?"

Thousands of Stanley Powells are equally confused. What about it? Is healing a possibility today? Do actual healings take place?

THE GIFTS OF HEALINGS

As long as Christians interpret the Scriptures from experience rather than interpret experience from the Scriptures, confusion will reign. In this chapter let's look at some facts from the Word of God that may help lift the fog.

When we use the phrase "the gift of healing," we normally think of physical healing. But the Greek language provides a different concept. While all the other gifts are referred to as *charisma* (singular), this gift is called *charismas* (plural), (1 Corinthians 12:9). Paul speaks of the gifts of healing rather than the gift of healing.

In fact, even the word "healing" is plural. Therefore, Paul refers to the *gifts of healings.*

I believe this means that some have the ability to heal the physically sick, others the gift to heal the emotionally sick, and others the gift to heal the spiritually sick. There is biblical evidence for each type of healing.

1. In Scripture, the word healing is used of *spiritual healing.* "For this people's heart is become gross, and their ears are dull of hearing, and their eyes they have closed, lest at any time they should see with their eyes, and hear with their ears, and should understand with their heart, and should be converted, and I should *heal* them" (Matthew 13:15). Further, Peter refers to spiritual healing like this: ". . . And He Himself bore our sins in His body on the cross, that we might die to sin and live to righteousness; for by His wounds you were healed" (1 Peter 2:24).

God uses gifted men and women to heal others of spiritual disease. When one person introduces another to Christ, spiritual healing takes place. Therefore, one who possesses the gift of evangelism also possesses the gift of spiritual healing. A pastor may lead a backslider into a vital relationship with Christ. That, too, is spiritual healing.

2. The Scriptures further speak of *emotional healing.* Early in his ministry, Jesus read from Isaiah and applied the Scripture to himself. "The Spirit of the Lord is upon me, because he hath anointed me to preach the gospel to the poor; he hath sent me to heal the brokenhearted, to preach deliverance to the captives, and recovery of sight to the blind, to set at liberty them that are bruised. . . ." (Luke 4:18). The word translated "brokenhearted" refers to those who are emotionally and mentally shattered. In fact, the last phrase of this quotation, "to set at liberty them that are bruised," also refers to emotional healing.

How desperately this gift of healing is needed today. Some Christian psychiatrists and psychologists have it. Counselors and pastors may also have it. This gift of healing is the ability to bring comfort and emotional stability to an individual who is going through emotional battles. It has been estimated that 50 percent of our hospital beds are occupied by those who have emotional problems. Billy Graham writes, "One out of every ten babies born today will be confined to a hospital with some form of mental illness at some time during his lifetime."[1]

3. Another kind of healing gift is the ability to heal people of their *physical illness.* This gift was demonstrated by our Lord and by some of his apostles. Jesus caused the deaf to hear and the blind to see. He gave speech to the dumb. He made it possible for the lame to walk. Those who lay sick with fever found relief. The paralytic took up his bed and walked.

Some of the apostles likewise used the gift of physical healing, though the gift is recorded only a few times in Acts. The first took place when Peter and John were walking into the temple. A man who had been lame from birth was placed there every day to beg for money. When he asked for money from Peter and John, Peter replied, " 'I do not possess silver and gold, but what I do have I give to you: In the name of Jesus Christ the Nazarene— walk!' And seizing him by the right hand, he raised him up; and immediately his feet and his ankles were strengthened. And with a leap, he stood upright and began to walk; and he entered the temple with them, walking and leaping and praising God" (Acts 3:6–8). See also Acts 5:16.

Another physical healing is recorded when Peter was traveling into Samaria to the city of Lydda. "And there he found a certain man named Aeneas, who had been bedridden eight years, for he was paralyzed. And Peter said to him, 'Aeneas, Jesus Christ heals you; arise, and make your bed.' And immediately he arose" (Acts 9:33, 34).

Philip was another one who had the gift of physical healing. "The multitudes with one accord were giving attention to retain what was being said by Philip, as they heard and saw the signs he was performing. For in the case of many who had unclean spirits, they were coming out of them shouting with a loud voice; and many who had been paralyzed and lame were healed" (Acts 8:6, 7).

Also recorded in Acts is a healing that took place when the Apostle Paul was shipwrecked. The entire crew was washed up

1 Billy Graham, *World Aflame* (Garden City, N.Y.: Doubleday, 1965), p. 26.

on the island of Malta. As they made their way through the island they discovered that the leader of the island was named Publius. Luke writes, "And it came about that the father of Publius was lying in bed afflicted with recurrent fever and dysentery; and Paul went in to see him and after he had prayed, he laid his hands on him and healed him. And after this had happened, the rest of the people on the island who had diseases were coming to him and getting cured" (Acts 28:8). See also Acts 14:9.

And so the Book of Acts records only three people who used the gift of physical healing: Peter, Philip, and Paul. They didn't often use the gift, but when they did, healing was instantaneous —without the use of medicine or medical skill.

Therefore, it's apparent that the gift of physical healing was rare even in New Testament times. One other fact of importance is that those who possessed this gift *used it sparingly.*

In 2 Corinthians 12:7–9 the Apostle Paul was afflicted physically. He wasn't able to use his gift to heal himself, nor did he receive healing when he prayed to God. He writes, "And because of the surpassing greatness of the revelations, for this reason, to keep me from exalting myself, there was given to me a thorn in the flesh, a messenger of Satan to buffet me—to keep me from exalting myself! Concerning this I entreated the Lord three times that it might depart from me. And He has said to me, 'My grace is sufficient for you, for power is perfected in weakness.' "

On another occasion, Paul's close friend and fellow-worker Timothy was ill with some type of stomach problem. Though Paul had the gift of healing, he refrained from healing his friend. He decided that Timothy should use what was available. "No longer drink water exclusively, but use a little wine for the sake of your stomach and your frequent ailments" (1 Timothy 5:23).

A further opportunity in which Paul might have used his gift of healing was the nearly fatal illness of his close friend Epaphroditus. "But I thought it necessary to send to you Epaphroditus, my brother and fellow-worker and fellow-soldier, who is also your messenger and minister to my need; because he was longing for you all and was distressed because you had heard that he was sick. For indeed he was sick to the point of death, but God had mercy on him, and not on him only but also on me, lest I should have sorrow upon sorrow . . . because he came close to death for the work of Christ, risking his life to complete what was deficient in your service to me" (Philippians 2:25–27, 30). God spared the life of Epaphroditus, but not by means of Paul's gift of healing.

During a terminal illness many Christians seek a "faith healer" as a last resort, hoping to save a loved one. Many believers cry to God for mercy so they won't have to face the agony of life without their life's partner, their child, or their friend. We hear about cancer patients now alive after doctors had given up hope. People are walking when they should be hopelessly paralyzed. Others regain their vision, though medical experience concludes they should be blind. All this leaves many Christians perplexed. Can God heal today? If so, does he heal today? Yes, he does.

God heals in a variety of ways

How simple it would be if God's methods were as unchangable as his character. But the Scriptures and experience inform us that our God is a God of variety.

1. God may heal *instantaneously.*

This is how we would like to program God. We hear of a miraculous, instantaneous recovery from serious illness. People are blessed. God is honored. Our faith is enlarged. And what happens? The next time a friend is seriously ill, we expect God to heal just as quickly. But as the days, weeks, and months pass, our faith is weakened. We begin to question God. We can't understand why he didn't heal our friend immediately.

Dr. R. A. Torrey, the great preacher of years past, has written about his own experience of this type of instantaneous healing: "How often God has given me faith as I have prayed for some sick one; and healing immediate, complete, and wonderful has followed."[2]

But God cannot be programmed. We cannot demand that he operate the same way in every case. God uses other methods of healing.

---

2 R. A. Torrey, *Divine Healing* (Grand Rapids: Baker Book House, 1970), p. 21.

2. God may heal *gradually.*

When I lived in Winnipeg, we asked two of the Winnipeg Blue Bomber football players to come out to our church gym and speak to our Athletic Teen Club. One of these professional players told about an experience that changed his Christian life. Benji Dial has a young son who was born with a deficiency in his spine. The doctors put him in braces. Months passed, but there was no improvement. As Benji and his wife began to search the Scriptures, they came to the conclusion that God not only could, but would heal their son. They prayed for his health. And then, as an act of faith, they removed the braces. The healing was not immediate, but as the weeks passed their son was restored to health.

Does this mean that if we had enough faith we could throw away all of our medicine and forget about the doctor? Not necessarily.

3. God may heal *through medication.*

In the Old Testament, King Hezekiah was told that he was going to die. He pleaded with God to spare his life. Then God promised to add fifteen more years to his life. After Isaiah brought the good news to Hezekiah he concluded by saying, "Let them take a cake of figs, and apply it to the boil, that he may recover" (Isaiah 38:21). I don't know what kind of healing power a cake of figs has, but it was the prescribed medicine here and it worked.

During our Lord's ministry he often merely touched a person for healing. But on one occasion he made a salve out of clay and spittle, and rubbed it on the eyes of a blind man. He commanded the blind man to wash his eyes, and when the blind man obeyed, his sight was restored.

Perhaps some of us would be in better health if we were to throw out the pills and drugs and other medicines we learn to depend upon almost to the point of addiction. But all medication isn't wrong.

I seldom use medicine for headaches. I have found that as I pray and meditate on God, my headache usually disappears. At other times, however, I use medication. God cannot be programmed. What we should strive for is balance in the Christian life.

God is a Spirit of variety. Since he has a unique plan for every one of his children, he doesn't treat us all the same. To one he gives excellent health. Why? Because that believer needs excellent health to fulfill God's plan for life. But God has a different plan for another child. That plan may include periods of long illness. He loves the second believer as much as the first, but he deals with him differently because his purpose is not the same for him.

What about faith? Can't we always expect God to heal if we really have faith? No, not necessarily.

1. God may withhold healing as a *discipline because of sin*. In Corinth there was a case of incest in the church. A man was living immorally with his stepmother. Paul warned, "I have decided to deliver such a one to Satan for the destruction of his flesh, that his spirit may be saved in the day of the Lord Jesus" (1 Corinthians 5:5). Apparently this man was stricken with an illness as a direct discipline for sin. Later, however, he did repent and Paul asked the church to restore him to fellowship (2 Corinthians 2:6–11).

A second instance of sickness as the result of sin is presented in 1 Corinthians. Some of the believers were partaking of the Lord's Supper in a disorderly manner. Paul writes, "Therefore whoever eats the bread or drinks the cup of the Lord in an unworthy manner, shall be guilty of the body and blood of the Lord . . . For this reason many among you are weak and sick, and a number sleep" (1 Corinthians 11:27, 30, NASB).

2. However, personal sin isn't the only reason for God's withholding the healing of the body. He may withhold healing for our *personal growth*. For instance, illness may add *humility* to our character (2 Corinthians 12:7–9).

Paul had a lot to boast about. He was well educated, he possessed an excellent Jewish religious heritage. He was zealous for God. He had seen the resurrected Christ, and then he had the privilege of seeing what heaven was like. What he saw was so marvelous he wasn't permitted to share his experience with others (2 Corinthians 12:4).

Paul could have gotten a "big head" because of these great experiences. He might have begun thinking that God favored him above all others. So he tells us that God permitted Satan to afflict him physically. God would not heal him. "And because of the surpassing greatness of the revelations, for this reason, *to keep me from exalting myself,* there was given me a thorn in the flesh, a messenger of Satan to buffet me—to keep me from exalting myself! Concerning this I entreated the Lord three times that it might depart from me. And He has said to me, 'My grace is sufficient for you, for power is perfected in weakness.' Most gladly, therefore, I will rather boast about my weaknesses, that the power of Christ may dwell in me. Therefore, I am well content with weaknesses, with insults, with distress, with persecutions, with difficulties, for Christ's sake; for when I am weak, then I am strong" (2 Corinthians 12:7–10).

I have observed over the years that no matter how brilliant or wealthy or popular or able a person is, God may provide some "thorn" to keep him humble. And this is a gracious act of God. If Paul hadn't been humbled by his illness, his ministry might have terminated early. Your "thorn" may be shortness of stature, big ears, an exaggerated nose, a throat ailment, a limp, or a deformity. Thank God for anything that keeps you from being exalted in your own eyes. Thank God that you recognize your limitations. For when you are weak in the flesh you can be strong in Christ.

It's easy for one to become complacent when he has good health. He begins to expect that good health is the norm and he takes it for granted. He starts to think God owes him good health. He may go about his daily routine giving lip service to God. But it's different when we are afflicted with disease. The body that once seemed limitless now becomes infected. We lie flat on our backs and remember the good times, the times of good health.

Several years ago, a close friend of mine broke four ribs. For months he fought to breathe without pain. After days and nights of agony God restored him to health. During a testimony meeting he said, "I thank God tonight that I am now able to breathe without pain." We *expect* to breathe without pain. But here was a man who could thank God with each breath that he had no pain.

Illness may add *empathy* to our character. Paul teaches us that affliction prepares us for service. "Blessed be the God and Father of our Lord Jesus Christ, the Father of mercies and God of all comfort; who comforts us in all our affliction *so that we may be able to comfort* those who are in any affliction with the comfort with which we ourselves are comforted by God" (2 Corinthians 1:3, 4). It isn't surprising that those who have tasted long illness desire to help others going through illness. They are capable of "feeling" with those who are sick.

3. Another possible reason why God doesn't always heal immediately or, at times not at all, is that he may receive greater glory in a person's sickness than in his recovery. Illness may *add to God's glory*.

When Jesus and his disciples had gone out of the temple one day, they spotted a man who was blind from birth. "And His disciples asked Him, saying, "Rabbi, who sinned, this man or his parents, that he should be born blind?' Jesus answered, 'It was neither that this man sinned, nor his parents; but it was in order that the works of God might be displayed in him.' " (John 9:2, 3). God didn't want this man healed early in life. He had his own timetable. And it wasn't until that very day that God was prepared to heal him.

Emily Gardiner Neal was an agnostic reporter who determined to expose the myth of healing. But in the process of her research she found Christ. She writes, "We are often led astray by the false assumption that God can be glorified only by a witness of physical healing. The truth is that some of the most effective Christian witnesses I know are those who are lying flat on their backs expectantly awaiting their healing by God's grace and at the same time are offering their suffering to be used for His glory."[3]

It's important to remember that in one situation God is glorified by healing. In another he is glorified by withholding healing.

God cannot be programmed. He cannot be confined to one purpose or one method. He is an unlimited God who is carrying out his purposes in our lives. Some of us remain sick when it is unnecessary. We should ask God to heal us. We should pray for the recovery of the sick. And if one has the gift of healing, he should use the gift as God leads. But if God says "no" as he said to Paul, or if he says "wait" as he did to the blind man, we should respond with rejoicing and thanksgiving. The ways of God are perfect.

3 Emily Gardiner Neal, *The Healing Power of Christ* (New York: Hawthorn, 1972), p. 22.

In his autobiography, Oral Roberts has written, "When healing comes, it is not simply because someone has a need. To me, the ultimate purpose of healing is to bring the person into a closer relationship to God and man. Healing is not an end in itself, but a means to an end—to be a better person and to do good in the world in which we live."[4]

Can we then say that when there is healing, the healing is always of God? No, for obvious reasons.

1. *All sickness is not the result of natural causes.* It's true that many of our illnesses come from a virus or the deterioration of some bodily organ. This is an organic cause. However there is also "psychosomatic illness." That is, illness induced by our emotions or by our imagination. The illness is real. The pain is real. People even die from psychosomatic illness. But the problem is with the emotions rather than the body.

Suppose you go to work one morning and as you arrive a fellow-employee says, "My, you must have had a rough night. You look beat." Actually, you had a good night and you feel great. But then a second and a third person tells you that you shouldn't work so hard. You should get more rest. You must be tired. By ten o'clock you begin to feel bushed. You look in the mirror and agree with everyone else, "Boy, I do look beat." Soon you feel shaky. Within minutes you're about to leave for home so that you can recover from your illness. That's psychosomatic.

Therefore, when people are healed, we can't necessarily conclude that it is a result of God's power, or the result of a believer who has the gift of healing.

2. Another reason why all healing is not of God is the *power of suggestion.* Dr. Ernest White states: "It is such people as these who, in despair of finding relief from ordinary medical means, turn to faith healing, or to Christian Science, or, in other cases, to unqualified practitioners of various kinds, and find relief or healing. One cannot deny that many people have been cured by various unscientific methods, and even by quacks and charlatans. In such cases, we must suppose that the healing agency has been

4 Oral Roberts, *The Call* (Garden City, N.Y.: Doubleday, 1972), p. 56.

the power of suggestion to which many people are particularly responsive."[5]

Since we are all subject to psychosomatic illness, we might do well to check when we get sick. Did our sickness come soon after a period of distress or pressure? If so, the same power of suggestion that made us sick could be reversed into a positive power to make us well again.

3. Another factor to consider is the *power of Satan.* What power heals people through witch doctors and those practicing white or black magic? Most likely it is the power of Satan. This power isn't new. The magicians of Moses' day were able to copy the first two acts of God's power, turning a stick into a serpent and making frogs come upon the land (Exodus 7:10–12; 8:5–7). Jesus said that there will be those at the judgment who say, "Lord, Lord, did we not prophesy in Your name, and in Your name cast out demons, and in Your name perform many miracles?" "And then I will declare to them, 'I never knew you; depart from Me, you who practice lawlessness' " (Matthew 7:22, 23). We are told that during the Great Tribulation there will be many false messiahs going throughout the world performing great miracles. "Then if any one says to you, 'Behold, here is the Christ,' or 'There He is,' do not believe him. For false Christs and false prophets will arise and will show great signs and wonders, so as to mislead, if possible, even the elect" (Matthew 24:23, 24).

Satanic power has been used in the past to mislead people. And it will be used in the future to deceive many. We can be certain that this power is now being used to heal people. It leads them into cults such as Christian Science, paganism, and occultism. If Satan can keep a man from Jesus Christ by healing his body, he'll be delighted to use that means.

However, some healing *is* of God. God at times steps into the impossible and brings forth a complete and immediate healing without medication. At other times he uses doctors and medicine to produce the same results.

But once again, remember that in every situation it isn't al-

5 Ernest White, *The Way of Release* (Ft. Washington, Pa.: Christian Literature Crusade, 1960), p. 77.

ways God's will to heal. You may have great faith, but after praying for a friend or someone in your family, you may see no results. You may be clean before God. You may plead to God. And yet, he may choose not to heal.

Oral Roberts explains that healing isn't a cut-and-dried process. "... There are many things about healing we do not know. In my brief experience I have prayed for some people with all the faith that I possessed and the person was not healed. In other instances, my faith was not as strong as I thought it should be and still the person was healed. I don't know how to explain that except to say there is only One who knows what is inside you and me and what it takes to really bring about a miracle. A doctor works with all the skill and compassion and faith at his command: some he helps, some he does not. It is the same way with prayer. Just as you have to draw strength from those you help and refuse to be discouraged when you fail, so must we continue our work in the face of both success and failure.

"There's no way to make praying for the sick easy. If the people who came only had minor afflictions—headaches, hay fever, or a cold—there would be no great risk.

"But when you say, 'I believe God heals,' and you're willing to be an instrument of God for healings, then you have to risk facing the worst possible cases—and failures. We've even had three people die during our crusades."[6]

What, then, about the gift of healing? Is it available for today?

the gift of physical healing is available for today

There is no biblical evidence that the gift of healing has been removed. Further, healings are taking place today. True, some healings may be the result of Satanic power. And others may be the result of the power of suggestion. But when some healings come from those who preach Christ and point people to Jesus, it is not a legitimate conclusion that they were only psychosomatic.

6 Roberts, *op. cit.,* pp. 52, 53.

Men like A. B. Simpson, Andrew Murray, and R. A. Torrey had little difficulty believing that God had used them on many occasions to heal the sick. And historically, the facts speak for themselves. Today, Oral Roberts has changed his emphasis from healing to preaching Christ. Nevertheless, he still believes that God has gifted him to heal and has seen positive results.

We need discernment for our times. Many "faith healers" bring dishonor to the Lord by their methods and exaggerated claims, but this is no reason to deny the validity of this gift as it is used properly. God has equipped men to touch us where it hurts.

CHAPTER FOUR

do you know where you're going?

The famous jurist Oliver Wendell Holmes once boarded a train but was unable to find his ticket. After watching him fumble through his pockets in growing dismay, the conductor said politely, "That's all right, Mr. Holmes; I'm sure you have your ticket somewhere. If you don't find it until you've gotten off, just mail it in to the railroad. We'll certainly trust you to do that."

Looking the conductor straight in the eye, Holmes replied, "Young man, that isn't my problem at all. I don't care about giving my ticket to the railroad; I just want to find out where in the blazes I'm going!"

Some churches, too, haven't the foggiest idea where they're going. God knows what happens when sheep are shepherdless and followers are leaderless. He has provided two gifts for the church to help it know where it's going as well as how to get there. Those gifts are leadership and faith.

THE GIFT OF LEADERSHIP

During the three years before he founded his Church, Jesus lived with a core group of twelve men. He taught, trained, and developed these disciples for leadership.

But these disciples had the same misconceptions about leadership that many Christians have today. They were overzealous for the glory and position, but gave little thought to the price. James and John in particular equated leadership with greatness. They asked Jesus to assign them positions next to him in his kingdom. Jesus' reply cut deeply to the heart of their motive. "You know that those who are recognized as rulers of the Gentiles lord it over them; and their great men exercise authority over them. But it is not so among you, but whoever wishes to become great among you shall be your servant; and whoever wishes to be first among you shall be slave of all" (Mark 10:42–44).

A significant principle is ignored when men strive for leadership in the church. Many seek the position but don't possess the gift. Christians must stop equating leadership with greatness. Leadership means opportunity to serve. Otherwise, divisions and contention result.

It's sad that after men work their way up the ecclesiastical ladder and finally become deacons, trustees, or elders, their effectiveness often declines. The "Peter Principle" works within church organization just as elsewhere: "A man tends to rise to his level of incompetence."

When the Church began at Pentecost the Holy Spirit came upon believers. He also imparted gifts, one of which was the gift of leadership. "And since we have gifts that differ according to the grace given to us, let each exercise them accordingly . . . he who leads, with diligence" (Romans 12:6a, 8c).

The word translated *lead* is from two Greek words meaning "before" and "stand." A leader is one who stands before others. He's out in front directing others toward a common objective.

common opinions about leadership

Many leaders fail because inadequate opinions about leadership prevail in their church.

1. Some tend to equate the gift of leadership with the *position*. Pastors wish this were true. If only people would automatically become leaders once elected to office! But experience demonstrates the fallacy of this. Often qualified people refuse to run for office while the incompetent grasp the opportunity for an

ego trip. Not all who hold a position of leadership possess the gift of leadership. Many church leaders are ungifted, untrained, and unteachable.

In one of my former churches we had a gifted man in a leadership position for several years. When he went off the board (by constitutional law), he remained the opinion setter. He continued to lead, primarily because of his high integrity. His position was gone but his gift still functioned. And because he wasn't threatened by the loss of position, he continued to lead effectively.

2. Others equate leadership with *personality*. They look to the extrovert, the "go-getter." It's true some extroverts gain the attention of a group for a period of time. But it's also true that some of these extroverts have as much ability as a passing hot east wind. They blow. They generate heat. But no one wants to follow them. Some of these people are self-appointed fruit inspectors. They enjoy taking the splinter out of a brother's eye. Others in this group are self-appointed critics. They feel called to point out what they see as wrong decisions of a church board or pastor. The extrovert is not always the best leader.

There is strong evidence that Timothy was an introvert. Yet he not only had a position of leadership, he also strongly influenced those with whom he associated.

Paul encouraged Timothy ". . . to kindle afresh the gift of God which is in you through the laying on of my hands. For God has not given us a *spirit of timidity,* but of power and love and discipline" (2 Timothy 1:6, 7). Though Timothy was a bit timid, Paul chose to send him to the Philippian church (Philippians 2:19). "For I have no one else of kindred spirit who will genuinely be concerned for your welfare . . . But you know of his proven worth. . . ." (Philippians 2:20, 22). When the Thessalonians needed to be built up spiritually, who was sent? "And so we send Timothy, our brother and God's fellow-worker in the gospel of Christ, to strengthen and encourage you as to your faith" (1 Thessalonians 3:2).

3. There are others who equate leadership with the *ability to speak.* But the gift of prophecy does not always come with the gift of leadership. For instance, the great duo that God sent to

Egypt consisted of a leader (Moses) and a spokesman (Aaron). There was no confusion in the minds of the people. Though Aaron did much of the speaking, they complained against Moses. In fact on one occasion even Aaron spoke against Moses the leader (Numbers 12).

4. One further misconception about the gift of leadership is that everyone who leads *must have the gift.* Certainly possessing the gift will make one a more effective leader. But the gift is not a prerequisite for all leadership responsibilities.

Though all of us are expected to give, we don't all possess the gift of giving. All of us are expected to witness, but we all don't possess the gift of evangelism. Likewise, in some sense all of us are leaders. The mother is a leader to her children. The husband is a leader in his home. And we all can learn certain skills of leadership and become more effective leaders, even though we may not possess the gift.

The person who possesses the gift of leadership will lead because it's "natural" for him. He'll experience definite results. People will want to follow him whether he's an elected official or not. When a job has to be done, his name pops into the minds of his peers.

uses of this gift

The gift of leadership may open the door for you to be elected to a church office such as elder/overseer or deacon (1 Timothy 3:1–13; Titus 1:5–9). You may find yourself chairing committees, emceeing meetings, or motivating groups to begin new projects. Young people may be using this gift as student council members or to serve on various committees. Women who have it may discover that they're consistently asked to lead women's projects or to be president of the Women's Missionary Society. They may be asked to sponsor the Pioneer Girls, the Awanas, or the Girl Scout program. Gifted men will have little difficulty finding places to serve in the church's Christian Education program. They may also use their gift on the boards of Christian schools, publication companies, evangelistic ministries, and other church-related services.

In *Leadership for Church Education,* Kenneth O. Gangel writes about the dynamics of spiritual leadership. He states that certain qualities demonstrate the uniqueness of spiritual leadership, including "faith, reliance upon prayer, the reality of the Holy Spirit in the life of the leader, and the absolute authority of God's inerrant Word as the basis for leadership."[1] Besides these obvious factors, other qualities mentioned by Gangel include dependability, meekness and humility, teachableness, and care of his followers.

selecting leaders

This gift is extremely practical. A wonderful spiritual revolution would take place in many churches if we would take this gift seriously. Could you imagine the blessings that would result from electing men to office on the basis of their gifts?

We would look for a man who has demonstrated the gift of leadership before placing him in the position of board chairman. No longer would we work on the assumption that because Mr. Jones has served so many years on the church board *we owe him* the office of chairman. Away with the idea that because a man was deacon for many years *he deserves* to become an elder. No longer would men who were faithful on the trustees board automatically be elected to the deacon board. Bury the warped philosophy that the faithful teacher must be chosen as Sunday school superintendent *because of many years of service.*

God has given gifts to men and he expects them to function in the appropriate capacities. It's therefore our responsibility to place gifted men and women in positions where their gifts can be used most effectively.

probing

A problem that inhibits some potential leaders from responsibility is the fear that leaders are born, not made. A person either has

1 Kenneth Gangel, *Leadership for Church Education* (Chicago: Moody Press, 1970), p. 174.

it or he hasn't. If he isn't born with leadership qualities, he avoids all leadership responsibilities. I would like to consider five questions:

1. Are leaders *born or made?*

Some people exhibit more natural leadership characteristics than others. They seem naturally able to gather a following. Though they've never had a course in leadership, some people have a "natural" instinct for leading. I believe that such individuals are stewards of the leadership gift. However, the gift does not automatically produce effective leaders.

I personally have never found it difficult to lead groups in various activities. I enjoy working with people. I experience a great sense of accomplishment when I help others in personal development. However, when I graduated from seminary, I quickly realized that to enjoy leading people wasn't enough. I was still ignorant of some basic leadership skills.

So I joined a Business Book Club. I bought selections that dealt with organizing, conducting meetings, planning proper use of time, decision-making, enlisting leaders and other skills. I read everything I could find in this general area. I attended leadership seminars. I listened to cassette tapes for managers and supervisors. Over the years I've discovered that what was within me by instinct was actually the gift of leadership. And it gradually matured and became refined.

Therefore in answer to the question whether leaders are born or made, I would have to say that those with the gift of leadership are born with the potential and will improve with training. Those without the gift can become effective within a more limited scope as they undergo training. A father can learn to become a better leader in his home but may not necessarily become a dynamic leader in the church.

2. Are *other gifts* usually associated with the gift of leadership?

As with all gifts, overlapping occurs. It is likely that each believer has several gifts. Because of the demands of leadership, the other gifts found with it could include wisdom, exhortation, prophecy, and faith.

3. Is it possible for two people to have the gift of leadership but *use it differently?* As an example, one leads like a one-man organization, while the other involves people.

Definitely. The gift doesn't determine its implementation. Many pastors have the gift of leadership and work better when they do all the work themselves. They may preach, teach, evangelize, visit, counsel, and chair the board meetings. Some pastors lead this way because they think that's their job. The congregation may agree. Some are one-man organizations because they feel threatened, others because they don't know how to enlist people to serve. Other pastors run the show because they're perfectionists at heart, who have little faith in the ability of others. They also fail to realize that God has gifted all men for service.

When such a man accepts God's philosophy of the local church (Ephesians 4:12), he has to change his method of leading. He no longer attempts to get others to help him do *his job*. Instead, he teaches others that the job of ministry is the responsibility of the congregation, while the task of the pastor is to equip the congregation to serve the Lord.

4. Can a person with this gift be *effective in one area of ministry and ineffective in another?*

As in the case of the gift of teaching, merely to possess the gift doesn't result in effectiveness wherever it's used. We are usually effective with people we know and understand. You may lead college students effectively because you've worked with them for several years. You know their frustrations, fears, questions, and potentials. But in a room of twenty junior high students you are tongue-tied and ill at ease.

Is this because you don't have the gift of "junior highers?" No. If you were to take the time to learn about junior high students, you could probably become as effective with them as you are with college students. The problem isn't the gift. It's lack of interest, experience, or making yourself available to understand how to use the gift elsewhere.

5. Is the gift of leadership recorded in Romans 12:8 identical with the gift of *"administration"* (1 Corinthians 12:8)?

Although the words are different, it probably refers to the

same *general* function of leading. Yet experience demonstrates that not all leaders are good administrators. The leader who does the work by himself and refuses to delegate responsibility isn't a good administrator even though he may get the job done. Administration is actually one aspect of total leadership responsibility. Administration has been defined as "getting things done *through people.*"

When Moses was bringing Israel from Egypt to the promised land he was leading them. But he wasn't a very efficient administrator. Moses's father-in-law, Jethro, saw the problem. He told Moses, "The thing that you are doing is not good. You will surely wear out, both yourself and those people who are with you, for the task is too heavy for you; you cannot do it alone . . . you shall select out of all the people able men who fear God, men of truth, those who hate dishonest gain; and you shall place these over them, as leaders of thousands, of hundreds, of fifties, and of tens. And let them judge the people at all times: and let it be that every major dispute they will bring to you, but every minor dispute they themselves will judge. So it will be easier for you, and they will bear the burden with you" (Exodus 18:17, 18, 21, 22).

A similar situation arose in the early church when the Hellenistic Jews had a dispute with the native Hebrews. The apostles were gifted leaders. And on this occasion they demonstrated that they also knew how to administrate. ". . . It is not desirable for us to neglect the Word of God in order to serve tables. But select from among you, brethren, seven men of good reputation, full of the Spirit and of wisdom, whom we may put in charge of this task. But we will devote ourselves to prayer, and to the ministry of the word" (Acts 6:2–4).

In a general sense, then, the gift of leadership (Romans 12:8) and the gift of administration (1 Corinthians 12:8) are identical. However, the gift of administration is probably a refinement of the general gift of leading.

As you try to understand whether you possess this gift or not, it would be to your advantage to take leadership courses, read books, and listen to cassettes. If your desire and ability to lead grow with responsibility and training, it strongly indicates that you have this valuable gift.

THE GIFT OF FAITH

When I was a teenager, I had the opportunity to earn some extra money working for a building contractor. They called me a "Contractor's Assistant." This meant that I carried the hammers, saws, and bricks, and mixed cement and dug ditches. During those weeks in the sticky Pennsylvania summer, it took all the discipline I could muster to stay on the job. As we insulated the roof, pieces of rock wool fell on my neck. The itching was driving me wild, and I made the mistake of scratching my neck. I forgot I had pieces of rock wool stuck to my fingers. I can still feel the prickling. I remember how I'd look at the contractor and ask myself, "What made him go into such a miserable business?" The yard was full of cinder blocks and cement. Piles of dirt decorated the front of the house, which itself was shapeless—nothing but beams and pieces of sheet rock lying around. I felt that the task was useless. How could my boss smile? Why didn't he mind the heat? Why didn't he give up when the house was so messy and the yard a junk pile?

Later in life I saw that the difference between the contractor and myself was vision. Because of his experience and his blueprints, he knew how the house would eventually look. The vision of a finished product motivated him to work in spite of the heat and humidity, and the early appearance of house and land. I, on the other hand, couldn't see the ultimate product. I hadn't had the experience of watching a house being built. My vision about the process was so limited that I failed to foresee the end result.

An interesting change in my attitude took place when the job neared completion. Wires were installed for electricity. Walls were erected. Shingles were put on the roof. A bulldozer leveled the dirt mounds. Another worker planted grass seed. Within weeks what had looked to me like utter chaos became a beautiful house on an attractively landscaped lot.

Both the contractor and I persevered to the end. But he ended as he began—optimistic, confident, and now proud of a job well done. I ended with a sense of relief. And I too was proud of the finished product. But because of my negative attitude and lack of vision, the job was twice as difficult as it needed to be.

the walk of faith

The Christian life parallels this experience. We all begin by faith (Ephesians 2:8, 9), but some people exercise little faith after they trust Christ for salvation. Their walk may be one of *feeling.* If they "feel" spiritual, they think they are. But if they have a hard day at the office, or feel discouraged, or frustrated, they conclude that their fellowship with God has been broken. Such persons wonder what sins they've committed, and may even end up with false guilt and defeat. (They should study the feelings of Jesus and consider how feelings and spirituality have little in common. Jesus wept (John 11:35); he felt grief (Matthew 26:38); he felt anger (Mark 3:5).)

Some Christians hear about being filled with the Holy Spirit (Ephesians 5:18) and ask the Holy Spirit to take over their lives. But after praying they expect "feeling," and the feeling doesn't come. No tingling, no goose pimples, no chill, no ecstacy. In disappointment they conclude that the Holy Spirit hasn't heard their prayer. Perhaps he has said, "No." And so again they attempt to live the Christian life in the power of the flesh.

Other believers walk by *sight.* They must see to believe. They look for signs and wonders, for the miraculous. They look for results, and if results aren't evident in a given time, they begin to doubt. "Maybe I'm not committed enough." (Paul said, "I have planted, Apollos watered, but God gave the increase." The increase will come, but in God's time and in God's way.)

The Christian life is a life of *faith.* "As you therefore have received Christ Jesus the Lord by faith, so walk in him by faith" (Colossians 2:6). "Without faith it is impossible to please Him" (Hebrews 11:6). "And whatever is not from faith is sin" (Romans 14:23).

The Christian who isn't walking by faith is like me when I worked for the contractor. He sees only the problems of life, the struggles and defeats. Without faith, adversity is problem-centered rather than potential-centered. Without faith, the future holds little hope for better things. Without faith, life is lived in the past and present, with little regard for the future. Without faith, the Christian life becomes stagnant.

the meaning of faith

Beyond the gift of saving faith (Ephesians 2:8, 9) and beyond the common faith we all are to exercise in the Christian life, lies the spiritual gift of faith. As Paul describes the Holy Spirit giving gifts to men he writes, "For to one is given the word of wisdom through the Spirit, and to another the word of knowledge according to the same Spirit; *to another faith* by the same Spirit" (1 Corinthians 12:8, 9a).

The writer to the Hebrews describes faith as "the assurance of things hoped for, the conviction of things not seen" (Hebrews 11:1). *The Living Bible* expands this description by stating that faith is "the confident assurance that something we want is going to happen. It is the certainty that what we hope for is waiting for us, even though we cannot see it."

Faith is taking God at his word and acting upon it. Faith is thanking God for what I believe he is going to do before he ever does it. Two weeks after my wife and I were married we moved from Lancaster, Pennsylvania, to Dallas, Texas. (We felt as though we were moving to the end of the world.) All our worldly possessions were able to fit in a 4' X 12' U-Haul trailer. When we arrived in Dallas we had about $250. It was the middle of summer. I was going to start school in the fall and my wife planned to teach, but in the meantime we tried to make our money stretch through two months. Neither of us could find a temporary job and our financial resources were dwindling.

I came to the conclusion that there was only one person who could help. Even though I was now married and wanted to be financially independent, circumstances demanded that I swallow my pride and ask for help. I made a long distance call to my father (reversing the charges, of course) and told him of my predicament. He seemed pleased with the request. He realized that the circumstances weren't the result of misusing our finances, and told me that a check would be in the mail.

My reaction was one of immediate peace. I had a need and I went to the one who I knew could meet it. Once my father guaranteed the answer, I no longer was concerned about the problem. The check didn't arrive for several days, because I had called on a weekend. But I didn't doubt my father's promise. I thanked him for his gift before he sent it.

Faith is like this. It's believing that our heavenly Father can and will supply our needs. Faith is asking God for what we need and then thanking him, even though the answer isn't yet at hand. Jesus said, "Therefore I say to you, all things for which you pray and ask, believe that *you have received them,* and they shall be granted you" (Mark 11:24).

the gift of faith

This is a special ability God gives to some believers to believe him for the "impossible." The person who possesses this gift has the ability to envision what God wants to accomplish in his life, his business, or his church. He also recognizes the obstacles that keep the average Christian from even asking God to fulfill that vision. Everyone else may sit back and say, "Let's use common sense. What you dream is impossible. It can't be done. There are too many problems." But the person with the gift of faith is not deterred.

When Robert Schuller determined to begin a drive-in church in southern California he encountered his greatest obstacles when he shared his vision with friends. He was both pitied and criticized. No one encouraged him, so Schuller reconsidered the idea. Was this vision from God or from an overactive imagination?

The week before he was to open his new drive-in church he attended Hollywood Presbyterian church. Dr. Ray Lindquist, preaching on Philippians 1:6 said, "God got you started in life, God has helped you to get where you are, and you can be sure that God will not quit on you." This was the encouragement Schuller needed. The next week his drive-in church opened, the Garden Grove Community Church. And today Robert Schuller holds seminars for hundreds of pastors around the country, using his gift of faith to encourage and challenge men who aren't using the faith they have.

Dr. Howard G. Hendricks gives an excellent example of the gift of faith working in the life of Dr. Harry Ironside. "Shortly after the seminary (Dallas Theological Seminary) was founded in 1924, it almost capitulated. It came to the point of bankruptcy. All the creditors were going to foreclose at 12 noon on a particular day. That morning the founders of the school met in the president's office to pray that God would provide, and in that prayer meeting was Harry Ironside. When it was his turn to pray, he prayed in his characteristically refreshing manner: 'Lord, we know that the cattle on a thousand hills are Thine. Please sell some of them and send us the money.'

"While they were praying, a tall Texan with boots on and an open collar came into the business office and said, 'I just sold two car-loads of cattle in Fort Worth. I've been trying to make a business deal go through and it won't work, and I feel God is compelling me to give this money to the seminary. I don't know if you need it or not, but here's the check.' A secretary took the check and, knowing the criticalness of the hour financially, went to the door of the prayer meeting and timidly tapped. When she finally got a response, Dr. Chafer took the check out of her hand, and it was for the exact amount of the debt. When he looked at the signature of the check, he recognized the name of the cattleman from Fort Worth. Turning to Dr. Ironside, he said, 'Harry, God sold the cattle.' "[2]

Dr. Ironside was a man gifted with faith. He knew God's Word and claimed its age-old promises for contemporary needs. Though the other men possessed faith and hoped that God would do something, Dr. Ironside expected God to provide the need.

2 Howard G. Hendricks, *Elijah: Confrontation, Conflict, and Crisis* (Chicago: Moody Press, 1972), pp. 19, 20.

getting it started and keeping it going

Pentecost really blew the minds of tradition-bound Jews at the close of that eventful Passover Feast (Acts 2). Jesus had given birth to his church. Like the wail of the newborn, the church's cry was heard through the streets of Jerusalem. The authority by which the young assembly spoke astounded the listeners. Three thousand souls responded to the cutting message (Acts 2:41).

But that day was unique. What guaranteed the genesis of other churches? And how would God provide for the new believers?

God solved these problems through four spiritual gifts: apostle, prophet, evangelist, and pastor-teacher. The first three get it started. The pastor-teacher then keeps it going. The former focus on birth. The last concentrates on growth.

THE GIFT OF APOSTLE

You may have a tendency to skip this chapter. After all, there's no way you could possess the gift of apostle, is there? You probably aren't even interested in becoming an apostle. It isn't practical. Perhaps it would be better to write just one paragraph about how the gift was used in the first century and then proceed to something more practical. After all, doesn't the Bible indicate that this gift has ceased along with the gift of prophecy? Didn't the great apostle himself write that the Church is "built upon the foundation of the apostles and prophets, Christ Jesus Himself being the cornerstone" (Ephesians 2:20)? (This means that our faith rests upon what they have said and written. In order to grow spiritually we turn to the Apostle Paul, the Apostle Peter, and the Apostle John for information).

It's true that in the restricted sense of the term the Apostles were the twelve plus a few others. Paul was an Apostle. Barnabas is also called an Apostle (Acts 14:14). Andronicus and Junias were outstanding Apostles (Romans 16:7). An Apostle was one who possessed some of the "sign" gifts (2 Corinthians 12:12; 1 Corinthians 14:18; Acts 2:43). He was called by God into his office (Romans 1:1). He was also a witness to the resurrected Christ (1 Corinthians 9:1; 1 Corinthians 15:5, 7, 8). In the order of gifts the gift of apostle leads the list (1 Corinthians 12:28). And as early as the end of the first century there were those who attempted to counterfeit the gift.

In the restricted sense the office and the gift of apostle have ceased. The foundation has already been laid. We need no new revelation (Galatians 1:12; 1 Corinthians 2:10). How then can we say that the gift of apostle is available for today? I believe that though one may not have seen the risen Christ, or received divine revelation, or demonstrated the sign gifts, in a general sense this gift has a contemporary application.

20th-century practices of 1st-century apostles

The word *apostle* comes from a Greek word meaning "to send." The apostle has a strong *sense of mission.* Paul's attitude was expressed when he wrote, "Woe is me if I preach not the gospel." The Apostles were men sent on a mission: to proclaim Christ to the world.

Another approach is to trace the type of ministry the Apostles had. In contrast to the evangelist, they spent a good deal of their time with Christians (Acts 2:42). In contrast to the pastor-teacher they also spent a lot of time with non-Christians (Acts 4:8). Their *ministry was evenly balanced.* Though Paul founded new churches throughout the East, he also went back over his former travels and built up the saints (Acts 14:21–23).

Further investigation provides another insight. After Paul started new works, he sent Timothy and Titus to go into the cities and build up his work. They were to build the work by organizing (Titus 1:5), teaching (Titus 2:1; 3:1) and shepherding the flock (Philippians 2:19–21). They were the pastor-teachers, building on Paul's foundation. But Paul refused to adopt that kind of ministry for himself. As an Apostle he declared, "And thus I aspired to preach the gospel, not where Christ was already named, that I might not build upon another man's foundation" (Romans 15:20).

Paul wasn't condemning building on what another man has started. He only says that his ministry differed. He traveled from one place to another, *starting new works*. In fact, Paul's longest recorded stay in any city was a period of three years, when he ministered to the Ephesian congregation (Acts 20:31).

Now when these qualities are compared with the ministry of some men today you find striking similarities. Package a sense of mission with a balanced ministry among Christians and non-Christians, and add the unique ability to begin new works. That is the history of many of our present-day Christian works, the modern missionary movement included. Today Livingstone and Africa, Judson and Burma, Carey and India are inseparably linked. Dawson Trotman and Torrey Johnson are impressed by God to establish a new work among servicemen. This results in two new works for God: The Navigators and Youth for Christ. A seminary student is impressed by God to reach the world's campuses for the Savior: Campus Crusade for Christ is born.

A similar union of interests and vision can be found in many pastors. In most pastoral ministries it's a good idea to remain in a church from four to eight years. If a pastor stays much longer he is looked upon with suspicion. "Is he planning to retire here? Has he found a comfortable job?" (Of course there are always the exceptions.) On the other hand, if a pastor moves too often, he is seen as immature or as an ecclesiastical ladder climber.

But suppose a pastor has the compulsion to be a "church planter." He goes to a city and starts a church. Then after one to three years, he leaves to begin a work in another city. This man should seriously consider the possibility that he may have the gift of apostle.

When I went to Winnipeg, Manitoba, for my first pastorate, I was told that two other men had preceded me. The first man had been there one year as pastor and the second man, eight years. On further investigation I discovered that the first pastor was the one who got the work started with the help of some local laymen. Before and after his Winnipeg ministry that pastor had started other churches. I met him at a conference and asked him why he pastored so many churches in such a short period of time. He replied that he felt this was the ministry to which God had called him.

the lay apostle

It's not unsual to find laymen with this gift of starting new works for the Lord. A layman may begin with one or several home Bible studies. He may then proceed to start a church from those studies. Another layman may attempt a ministry through literature, radio, or TV.

Perhaps you sense this pioneer spirit in yourself. You may want to begin a work that no one else has attempted. You don't want to build on another man's foundation. God may have given you a vision to launch out into a new area of ministry that scares you now. You've never tried it. No one has ever done it before. Before you decide to give it up as a lost cause, consider the fact that you may have this gift. Launch out. Attempt great things for God. Another apostle once said as he faced the impossible, "I can do all things through Him who strengthens me" (Philippians 4:13).

THE GIFT OF PROPHECY

Of all the spiritual gifts Paul mentions he spends most time dealing with the gifts of tongues and prophecy. Tongues were being abused, and prophecy was being neglected. Tongues were emphasized while prophecy was deemphasized. To correct the problem, the apostle discusses at length the priority of gifts, especially encouraging prophecy.

Some excerpts from 1 Corinthians 14 reveal the value of prophecy. "Pursue love, yet desire earnestly spiritual gifts, but especially that you may prophesy . . . one who prophesies edifies the church . . . greater is one who prophesies than one who speaks in tongues . . . since you are zealous of spiritual gifts, seek to abound for the edification of the church . . . prophecy is for a sign to those who believe . . . desire earnestly to prophesy" (verses 1, 4, 5, 12, 22, 39).

What is the gift of prophecy? Is it the gift that Jeane Dixon claims to have?[1] Is it fortune-telling? Does it have anything to do with astrology or horoscopes? Is it revival preaching?

In the Scripture, the prophet was one who understood God's revelation and correctly interpreted it to others. "Prophecy" comes from two Greek words meaning "to shine before." When the prophet speaks he is like a lamp shining in a dark place (2 Peter 1:19).

Both the Old and New Testament prophets would receive a revelation from God and then proclaim and interpret it to others. Or (as in the case of Peter who already had some of God's revelation in written form) he interpreted the Old Testament in light of current events: "Men of Israel, listen to these words: Jesus the Nazarene . . . you nailed to a cross . . . and God raised Him up again, since it was impossible for Him to be held in its power. For David says of Him (quote from Psalm 16:8–11). . . . Brethren, I may confidently say to you regarding the patriarch David that he both died and was buried, and his tomb is with us this day. And so, because he was a prophet, and knew that God had sworn to him with an oath to seat one of his descendants upon his throne, he looked ahead and spoke of the resurrection of the Christ, that He was neither abandoned to Hades, nor did His flesh suffer decay. This Jesus God raised up again, to which we all are witnesses" (Acts 2:22–25, 29–32).

prediction

As a prophet, David predicted the resurrection of Christ one thousand years in advance. The test of any prophetic ministry is

1 See *Satan Is Alive and Well on Planet Earth,* Hal Lindsey, pp. 114–128.

whether the prediction comes true. Anyone who claims to be a prophet in this sense must be 100 percent accurate. If he or she fails at any point, we must conclude that the prophecy and the prophet do not come from God. "When a prophet speaks in the name of the Lord, if the thing does not come about or come true, that is the thing which the Lord has not spoken. The prophet has spoken it presumptuously; you shall not be afraid of him" (Deuteronomy 18:22).

The test for true and false prophets is available for all of us to use. The Apostle John warns every Christian, "Beloved, do not believe every spirit, but test the spirits to see whether they are from God; because many false prophets have gone out into the world" (1 John 4:1). But in spite of that warning, some people get excited when they hear of a prophet who is even partially accurate.

proclamation

The other ministry of a prophet was to proclaim God's revelation. Peter fulfilled this aspect of the prophetic ministry by proving from the Old Testament that Jesus of Nazareth was the Messiah. Peter compared God's truth with current events, and then accurately applied truth to life.

Some New Testament prophets were Barnabas, Simeon, Lucius, Manaen (Acts 13:1), Judas, and Silas (Acts 15:32). There were also women who prophesied throughout the first century. Anna is called a prophetess (Luke 2:36). When Jesus was brought to the temple by his parents to be presented to the Lord, Anna "came up and began giving thanks to God, and continued to speak of Him to all those who were looking for the redemption of Jerusalem" (Luke 2:38). Women in the early church were told that their prophesying should be done with their heads covered (1 Corinthians 11:5). Philip the evangelist had four unmarried daughters who were prophetesses (Acts 21:9). The latter days are to see a resurgence of this gift among men and women (Acts 2:17).

What have we learned so far? We have seen that a prophet could predict future events with complete accuracy and/or he could interpret God's truth and relate it to life. Further, the gift of prophecy wasn't limited to men. What the prophets received from God was written and guarded over the years, and therefore Paul could say that the church is built upon the apostles and prophets (Ephesians 2:20).

These prophets received their messages from God and then proclaimed them to others. Sometimes the messages were from written revelation, as when Peter quoted from the Old Testament law, Psalms and prophets (Acts 2, 3). At other times the message was a new revelation. Eventually these messages were recorded. You and I benefit from them today when we read the New Testament. If God is giving new information today in the form of a prophecy it is in keeping with whatever he previously gave to the early church. Anyone who claims to have a new revelation from God that contradicts the Scriptures has an invalid source of revelation.

The gift of prophecy is available today, though, like the gift of apostle, it takes on a different form. God is no longer adding to his inspired Word. John, who was both an apostle and prophet wrote, "I testify to everyone who hears the words of the prophecy of this book: if anyone adds to them, God shall add to him the plagues which are written in this book" (Revelation 22:18). However, the need is great for men and women to read, interpret, and proclaim the truth that God has revealed.

the value of prophecy

But what can you expect from this gift? God isn't predicting future events through his prophets today; all the necessary prophetic truth has already been written, so what value does the gift of prophecy have?

The value of the gift is given in 1 Corinthians 14:3, "But one who prophesies speaks to men for edification and exhortation and consolation." The major responsibility of the gift of prophecy today is to study and interpret the Word of God so that believers experience spiritual growth, spiritual discipline, and spiritual encouragement.

1. This gift may be demonstrated in *preaching*. When a preacher faithfully studies the Word of God and then stands be-

fore a congregation and preaches, he may be using the gift of prophecy. If the congregation is edified, encouraged, or comforted there is evidence that he possesses the gift. It would be wonderful if every ordained preacher possessed the gift of prophecy, but experience and Scripture demonstrate that this isn't the case. Perhaps you've been sitting under the ministry of a man who doesn't seem to possess this gift. This doesn't mean he's not a man of God, and you shouldn't conclude that he doesn't belong in the pastorate. It may be that he just doesn't possess the gift of prophecy. (In many churches, a man is called for every reason under the sun except for his gifts. Some congregations want a teacher but hire a preacher [gift of prophecy]. Some want an evangelist but hire a teacher [gift of pastor-teacher]. Some want a preacher but hire an administrator [gift of administration].)

2. This gift may also be used in *writing*. Where the gift of teaching might be used in writing Sunday school curriculum, the gift of prophecy may be used in writing magazine articles, newspaper articles, or books. You may use your gift on the school newspaper to speak out for Christ. Or you might want to submit articles to your denominational magazine, as you write about meaningful Christian living as a housewife or from the standpoint of a working woman. One mother had a message to share with the world after she went through a soul-searching experience, and thousands of other parents are benefiting as they read *Eighteen and No Time to Waste*.

Perhaps as you read this book you feel that you have something to say. God has given you fresh insight into his Word that has changed your life. You're not a public speaker, you're not a professional writer, and therefore you've kept the message to yourself. I encourage you to write down what is on your heart. Ask God to open the doors if he wants to get the message out. Publishing companies aren't looking only for the professional writer. They're looking for people who have a message.

3. A friend of mine discovered a way to use his prophetic gift in *films*. As students in seminary he and I spent hours talking about the great TV and film productions we would some day make. He was working at a local TV station at the time and encouraged me

to get a job with him. Since my master's thesis was to be written about television I thought that this would provide excellent background. I took the job. But after graduation our paths separated. My gifts were being developed in the field of Christian education and later in a pastoral ministry. My friend, however, used his gifts in writing for a popular Christian magazine. Then he pastored for a few years, taught in a Bible college, and finally found another medium for his message, films. During the past few years he has been developing a new ministry, The Evangelical Communications Research Foundation. So far his messages have gone forth through such films as "The Emerging Church," "The Long Way Back," "The Walls of Time" with Ken Taylor, and "The Return" with Hal Lindsey.

You don't have to be an ordained minister or a seminary graduate to use this gift. If you find it enjoyable to speak in public it's possible that God has given you the gift of prophecy. At times you may use this gift in church, rescue missions, or service clubs. You may speak to women's groups or to children. If you begin to get feedback that people have been blessed by your ministry, be encouraged. You may not be able to exposit in depth like a teacher. You may not have people respond like an evangelist. But if people are comforted, encouraged, and spiritually strengthened by your ministry, it's probable that you possess the gift of prophecy.

It's imperative not to limit God to a certain method or medium through which he wants to use the gift of prophecy. He isn't limited to professionals when he wants to dispense it, and you may be one of his contemporary prophets.

THE GIFT OF EVANGELISM

Christianity is one of the few world religions that was founded on evangelism: the proclamation of good news. From its beginning, Christianity was to go into all the world without racial, sexual, or economic distinction. Paul said, "Or is God the God of Jews only? Is He not the God of Gentiles also? Yes, of Gentiles also" (Romans

3:29). "There is neither Jew nor Greek, there is neither slave nor free man, there is neither male nor female; for you are all one in Christ Jesus" (Galatians 3:28).

Because the message is essential for the entire world to hear, Jesus provided for its propagation in two ways. He commanded every believer to be a witness of his saving power (Acts 1:8), and then he gave certain believers the gift of evangelism in order to bring the multitudes to himself. "And He gave some . . . as evangelists" (Ephesians 4:11).

What is an evangelist? Is he one who preaches to large crowds? Must he be an ordained minister? Is it possible for a layman to be an evangelist?

Actually the Bible tells us very little about the evangelist, but speaks often about evangelism. The term *evangelist* comes from a root word translated "gospel" or "good news." It is used only three times in the Scriptures. Besides the Ephesian passage, the word is used to describe a man named Philip. "And on the next day we departed and came to Caesarea; and entering the house of *Philip the evangelist,* who was one of the seven, we stayed with him" (Acts 21:8). Philip is the only man in the Bible who is called an evangelist. Peter and Paul were apostles. Timothy and Titus were pastors. Agabus was a prophet. But Philip has the distinction of being called "the evangelist."

Philip was one of the original seven chosen to take care of the daily distribution in the church at Jerusalem (Acts 6:1–6). The Bible does not say if he was preaching at this time. But as he served the Lord faithfully in the distribution of supplies out of the common treasury, opportunities became available to preach Christ. He and the other believers continued to share their faith. Soon the religious leaders determined to put an end to this new religion, and within weeks this growing menace to Jewish tradition had its first martyr, Stephen (Acts 7). This was the end of normal life for a Christian living in Jerusalem. A great persecution swept through the houses and streets of the "holy city."

Led by the Jewish fanatic, Saul of Tarsus, men and women were dragged from their houses and thrown into prison (Acts 8:1–3). Many Christians fled from the city and headed into Judea and Samaria. And as they took up residence in new regions they "preached the word." They *evangelized*. Acts 8 reveals that the apostles did not go into the regions evangelizing. They stayed in Jerusalem (Acts 8:1). It was the laymen who went about evangelizing.

The Bible next moves from the general to the specific and mentions one of these laymen, Philip. "And Philip went down to the city of Samaria and began proclaiming Christ to them" (Acts 8:5). This passage provides insight into the ministry of an evangelist.

1. His service was *itinerant*. Philip wasn't pastoring a church. He was traveling and stopped at Samaria for a short period of time, perhaps a few weeks. Later he moved on into Gaza in south Palestine (Acts 8:26). He led one man to Christ at that point and then went on to Azotus (formerly Ashdod). The last mention of Philip (until Acts 21:8 where he was in Caesarea) is this: "But Philip found himself at Azotus: and as he passed through he kept preaching the gospel *to all the cities,* until he came to Caesarea" (Acts 8:40).

2. Another insight into the evangelist's ministry concerns *the people* to whom he preaches. Philip was preaching to unbelievers. The Samaritans weren't Christians. They were a mixture of Jew and Gentile, with a religion similar to the Jews'. They, too, were expecting the Messiah to come (John 4:25), yet they were convinced that God should be worshiped in Mount Gerizim rather than at Jerusalem (John 4:20). These people were religious, but needed to be evangelized with the gospel.

3. The third distinction of the evangelist is *his message*. Philip wasn't building up the saints. He wasn't teaching believers the whole counsel of God, as Paul would have done. Philip had one primary message on his heart. When he preached to the Samaritans he told them about "the good news about the kingdom of God and the name of Jesus Christ" (Acts 8:12). When Philip preached to the Ethiopian he "opened his mouth, and beginning from this Scripture [Isaiah] he preached Jesus to him" (Acts 8:35).

4. A fourth characteristic of the evangelist is *his results*. Philip preached Christ to the unbelieving Samaritans, "and the multitudes with one accord were giving attention to what was said by Philip . . . *they believed* Philip preaching the good news" (Acts

8:6, 12). Likewise, when Philip preached Christ to the Ethiopian, he believed.

Look again at these distinctions from a different perspective. If you were to compare the ministry of the evangelist with the ministry of the prophet or preacher you would discover the following contrasts.

evangelist vs. pastor-teacher

1. The *message* of the evangelist is primarily the gospel: Christ died for our sins, was buried, was resurrected from the dead the third day. The message centers around the person of Jesus Christ. The message of the pastor-teacher is more varied. His message includes more of "the whole counsel of God." He may preach about the Church as the body of Christ. He may emphasize spiritual gifts, temptations, prayer, mental health, the Christian home, stewardship, etc. He may preach about angels and demons.

2. The *method* of the evangelist is to go where unbelievers are. This may include traveling from city to city, church to church, campus to campus, house to house, or person to person. He reaches out. The emphasis is on an itinerant ministry. In contrast the pastor-teacher remains at one place for a much longer period of time. His message can't be preached in one night or even in one month.

3. A third contrast between the evangelist and pastor-teacher is found in his *purpose*. The purpose of the evangelist is to win men to Christ. The purpose of the pastor-teacher is to build men and women in the faith. The one looks for a new birth while the other looks for spiritual growth.

4. A final contrast between the gifts of evangelism and pastor-teacher centers around the *results*. When a person has been affected by an evangelist he turns from darkness to light, from spiritual death to spiritual life. When a man responds to the ministry of the pastor-teacher he grows in his spiritual life. He may be encouraged or comforted.

It's important to understand that I'm referring to the emphasis of ministry. Just as an evangelist may pastor a church, so some pastors may travel a lot. Some evangelists may preach on a variety of subjects and some pastors may limit their preaching to John 3:16. You may discover certain evangelists dealing with young Christians and helping them grow. On the other hand some pastors may continuously spend time attempting to win unbelievers to Christ. But as a general rule you find that the evangelist's emphasis differs from the pastor's.

questions

1. Perhaps you're wondering whether the gift of evangelism is limited to those who have had *formal Bible training or who are ordained* evangelists. Could it be possible that you, a student or layman, may have this gift?

Certainly it's possible. Recently in my home church in Lancaster, Pennsylvania, a group of lay witnesses came to share what Jesus Christ meant to them. During several days of sharing the reality of Christ, a number of the people came into a personal relationship with Christ. Many of the Christians experienced a newness of the Holy Spirit. The pastor stated that he was like a new person. Today the church is filled with life, enthusiasm, and a sense of unity. They had to set aside a Saturday evening in order to baptize those who came to Christ. Interestingly, during the past twenty-five years or more this church annually had evangelists come and go, but the results were few. What the professionals couldn't accomplish, the laymen did. God chose to use laymen to perform great works.

2. Is it possible for a *woman* to possess the gift of evangelism?

Yes. When I was a student at Dallas Theological Seminary I worked on the part-time staff of Campus Crusade for Christ. At that time there were about 250 staff, many of them young women. It was a policy of Crusade that men were to witness to men and women were to witness to women. Therefore, the majority of the college women who came to Christ did so through the female staff of Crusade.

Recently a young woman of our church let it be known that she was available to speak at evangelistic teas. Another young lady responded by personally inviting seventy-four women to her house for the tea. Twenty-three attended. When the speaker extended an invitation to these women, six of them responded. While the one woman used her gift of helps for an evangelistic purpose, the other used her gift of evangelism for the same objective. Both were doing the work of evangelism, and God blessed their faithfulness.

3. How can I know *whether I have the gift* of evangelism?

This question will be covered in more detail in chapter 11. However, if you can answer two questions affirmatively, it's quite possible that you possess this gift. First, do you have a strong desire to share your faith with others? I'm not asking whether you want to see people come to Christ. Most Christians want to see a life changed. But do you personally enjoy talking to others about Christ? A second question is, are you seeing results? Are people coming to Christ in your ministry? When I worked with Campus Crusade I used to become frustrated. I would hear about other staff workers introducing students to Christ, and I would compare their results with mine. They always saw greater numerical results. I searched my heart before God. Was I lacking faith? No, because some responded to my ministry. But again they were the exception. My batting average was extremely low. Was my message deficient? No, I gave the same "Four Spiritual Laws" that all the other staff workers gave. Even today, after serving in three churches, I still see few people coming to Christ in spite of the fact that the message is clear.

I must therefore decide that either I am a complete failure as a minister or that my gifts are in an area other than evangelism. Experience has demonstrated greater results from my pastor-teacher gift. The Bible reveals that just as the Holy Spirit gave *some* pastor-teachers, he also gave *some* evangelists. And as we all don't have the gift of pastor-teacher, we all don't have the gift of evangelism.

4. Could I have the gift of evangelism and yet be more proficient *using it* in one way than another?

Yes. Some people are quite successful using their gift on the college campus but became almost useless when working with children. Others are great in personal evangelism but become weak-kneed and tongue-tied when speaking to large groups. One person may be successful using his gift with groups such as in a home Bible study, and yet tremble at the thought of going door-to-door. Those who work with children aren't necessarily so proficient when ministering to adults.

It's a shame when spirituality is judged on the basis of "How many souls have you won? What! Only a handful? Come now, brother. Don't you think you'd better get right with God?" Perhaps one should reply to such an inquiry: "How many Christians have you helped to grow in their spiritual life? What? Nobody has grown spiritually? Don't you think you'd better get right with God?" You see, whether it's the gift of evangelism or the gift of teaching, both come from God and are to be used for his glory. The question of spirituality must be decided on the basis of whether one is using *his* gift in the power of the Holy Spirit, not whether he has won hundreds to Christ.

5. *Where* should I use my gift of evangelism?

I suggest that you use your gift in as many areas as possible. As time progresses you will begin to find greater enjoyment and greater results in some areas and less enjoyment and results in others.

Few laymen realize that they have open doors that are closed to the clergy. The student has school. The mechanic has his shop. The housewife has her unchurched friends. The businessman has his associates. The minister is limited primarily to the church buildings, unless laymen open the door for him in their areas of influence.

6. If I don't have the gift of evangelism should I bother to *witness?*

Definitely. Jesus said, "You shall be my witnesses" (Acts 1:8). Earlier he said, "You are witnesses of these things" (Luke 24:48). To what was he referring? "Thus it is written, that the Christ should suffer and rise again from the dead the third day; and that repentance for forgiveness of sins should be proclaimed in His name to all the nations, beginning from Jerusalem" (Luke 24:46, 47).

They were witnesses of the gospel. If you have experienced forgiveness of sins through Jesus Christ, you have something to talk about. If you have been changed by the power of God, you have a message to share. Anyone who takes training from a Campus Crusade staff worker will be told, "A successful witness is making the way of salvation clear, giving the person an opportunity to respond, and leaving the results up to God." God hasn't called us to save people. He has called us to witness, to share with another what Christ has done for us.

Paul encouraged Timothy in his second letter, "But you, be sober in all things, endure hardship, *do the work of an evangelist, fulfill your ministry*" (2 Timothy 4:5). The work of an evangelist is to inform men that though God truly loves them, their sin separates them from him. The only way to resolve the sin problem and to build a relationship with God is to accept the provision God has made: the perfect sacrifice, Jesus the Christ. To reject God's provision is to reject the only hope man can have for personal salvation.

No, the gift of evangelism isn't given to everyone. But all of us are commanded to witness. Though men always look for results, God is primarily concerned with man's faithfulness. Men reward on the basis of results. God rewards on the basis of faithfulness, for he is the one who gives results.

The person gifted with evangelism will see many results and be rewarded because he was faithful. He who lacks the gift will see fewer results, but will likewise be rewarded because he too was faithful in his witness. Paul told the Corinthian believers, "Let a man regard us in this manner, as servants of Christ, and stewards of the mysteries of God. In this case, however, it is required of stewards that one be found trustworthy" (1 Corinthians 4:1, 2).

THE GIFT OF PASTOR-TEACHER

Have you come across any frustrated ministers recently? There are plenty. A university professor told me that his speech department is full of former ministers. Some are now teachers. Others are students. Go to your local TV station and you may find a former minister giving the weather report. There were three former ministers at the TV station where I worked as a seminary student.

Why the ministerial dropout? Possibly because some have never been called by the Lord. They may have been pushed by well-meaning parents. Perhaps they were exhorted by a minister who was keeping a record of how many young people he led into the ministry. But they never heard the still, small voice of God. Others got tired of living on starvation wages. Some became discouraged when the "resistance movement" (to new ideas and methods) blocked progress.

the office of pastor-teacher

But there is another reason for a minister's frustration and eventual dropout: the confusion between pastoral office and pastoral gift. Either the minister, or the congregation is confused, or both. Meet four frustrated ministers.

Allan Anderson has the gift of evangelism. He has seen several hundred people come to Christ. He introduced some of them to Jesus on a man-to-man basis. Others responded to his invitation Sunday mornings. His congregation appreciates his appeal to the lost, but many of them are still "babes in Christ." Some complain that they are starving for spiritual food. Some older members complain that though he visits the lost with fervent zeal, he neglects *them*. Mr. Anderson is frustrated because his people need spiritual food while he wants to preach to the lost. Should he stay at his church and be frustrated? Or would it be better to venture out into a ministry of evangelism where he really would be at ease?

Frank Foreman has been in his church for about four years. When he first came, the people loved him. He was a great organizer. The church was in chaos four years ago, but today it runs like a well-oiled engine. Yet the congregation lacks the enthusiasm they had under their former minister. He was so warm, so concerned for people. He was Johnny-on-the-spot when anyone needed anything. True, everything was hectic. The former minister's philosophy was "play it by ear." He never thought about long-range planning, setting goals, or evaluating present programs. He just preached and visited and loved people. Mr. Foreman has heard his predecessor's record played over and over. But now he's tired, frustrated, and ready to quit.

The minister at the Community Church seems to be an exception. There are all kinds of activities during the week. Children's groups meet Monday; teens, Thursday. Adults have their regular Wednesday meeting followed by choir rehearsal. Everything looks exciting from outside the church. But an hour at the board meeting tells it differently. "We're being exhorted to death," claims one board member. "We've been challenged to visit, witness, teach, and get saved. But none of us know how to do anything. We have no training. No one tells us how. No one takes us out and shows us what to do. We're exhorted to come to prayer meeting, but when we come there's nothing but more exhortation. Sam Smith is a wonderful man. We all love him. But there has to be something more to the Christian life than an endless call to battle the enemy." Mr. Smith was shocked to hear this accusation. And when there was general agreement with what was said, he was ready to leave.

The story of Ernest Elliot is different. He's a gifted teacher. He's written several books. His name is familiar throughout the country. But in his own church he has experienced the proverb, "A prophet is without honor in his own country." Dr. Elliot isn't a stimulating speaker. In fact, his membership has decreased over the years because his messages sound like university lectures. The college crowd loves him, but they don't pay the bills. The church has been running in the red for the past three years, and even had to cut Dr. Elliot's salary this past year. Frustration, hurt feelings, and deep depression are becoming a way of life for this minister.

the problems

Many congregations expect all ministers to be alike. When the new one differs from the former, he is suspect. Seldom does a congregation choose a man on the basis of his gifts. They tend to judge from his sermon or appearance. Some congregations just want to get a vacancy filled, but as soon as the new man doesn't meet their expectations the grumblers begin.

Adding to that problem, many ministers choose churches on the basis of their location, salary, and prestige. Some may even accept a position because they want to escape the problems of their present ministry. Seldom do ministers accept a call by determining how their gifts will meet the needs of the new church.

The result? Men of God hold the office of pastor, but don't have the gift of pastor-teacher. Mr. Anderson's gift is evangelism. He loves the Lord. He sees results. But his people aren't satisfied. Mr. Foreman's gift is administration. His church is one of the leading churches of the city for "program." He has provided fantastic leadership in Christian education, but his people still complain. Mr. Smith has the gift of exhortation, but his people are tired of being told what to do. Dr. Elliot is gifted as a teacher, but his church is poorly organized. Bills aren't paid. No one has come to Christ for several years.

What could be done to help these men remain in the ministry and still find fulfillment in life?

let's keep our ministers

Both pastor and congregation should understand the purpose of the local church. If the local church is a soul-saving station, it should employ those who have the gift of evangelism. Then the people can bring the lost into the building and the preacher can "get them saved."

If the local church is primarily an organization made up of program and people, it should employ those gifted in administration. A good administrator can enlist workers and set up organizational procedures so that a church will function efficiently.

If the church is primarily called to perform certain religious activities, then a congregation would be wise to hire one gifted with exhortation. He could then challenge the members to get busy for God. "Get involved!" "Get moving!"

If the church is basically a center of learning, we need to find a great teacher. He will come into the building and impart biblical facts. The heads of believers will be filled, even though their hearts may be empty.

But the church isn't primarily a soul-saving station, an organization, a center of religious activity or learning. It's more than all of these. The Bible describes the purpose of the local church like this: Gifted men such as pastor-teachers have been given to the local church "for the equipping of the saints for the work of service, to the building up of the body of Christ" (Ephesians 4:11, 12).

The pastor has been called by God to equip the saints ("called-out ones"). The saints have been called for the work of service. And when the pastor does his job and the saints do their job, the local body of Christ will be built up. The word "equip" is used in the Gospels to describe "mending torn nets." Sometimes the pastor has to mend broken hearts and broken relationships. It also means "to complete what is lacking."

The work of service which the people accomplish includes evangelism, teaching, visiting, disciplining, caring for others, building equipment, driving Sunday school buses, singing, etc. Once this is understood, the pastor and his congregation should think of themselves as a team. What the pastor lacks in gifts, someone in the congregation may have. Or the church may consider hiring a man to complement the pastor's gifts. If the pastor has the gift of teaching but lacks the gift of administration, someone from the church may be able to use his gift of administration effectively on the church board. But for this to succeed, both pastor and people must understand the church's function and must also be secure in themselves. The Body of Christ will operate effectively as all of the gifts are used together: the gifts of the pastor to equip the people, the gifts of the people to serve the Lord. For a more complete understanding of the church operating as a body, I encourage you to read *Body Life* by Ray C. Stedman.[2]

How can we keep ministers in the ministry? First we must understand that one may hold the office of pastor without possessing the gift of pastor-teacher. Second is to develop the team ministry of complementary gifts, such as the pastor and his people and/or the pastor and another staff worker.

2 Ray Stedman, *Body Life* (Glendale, Calif.: Regal Books, 1972).

biblical examples

The pastor-teacher is a combination of two gifts. The gift of pastor refers to the ability to care for another. Like a shepherd, he cares for his sheep. The second gift explains how the shepherd cares. He uses the gift of teaching. The individual who possesses this gift is a teaching pastor.

Spiritual shepherds are found in both the Old and New Testaments. Ezekiel was sent to prophesy against the shepherds of Israel. "Prophesy and say to those shepherds, 'Thus says the Lord God, woe, shepherds of Israel who have been feeding themselves! Should not the shepherds feed the flock?" (Ezekiel 34:2). As God continues to warn these unfaithful shepherds, we get an insight into the ministry of a shepherd.

He is to feed his flock (34:2). He should strengthen the sick and heal the diseased, bind up the broken, bring back the wandering, seek the lost (34:4), and lead them to rest (34:15). He protects them from their enemies (Psalm 23:4, 5).

The New Testament describes the ministry of pastoring in greater detail. The Apostle Peter calls Jesus the Chief Shepherd (1 Peter 5:4). The writer to the Hebrews calls the Savior the great Shepherd (Hebrews 13:20). Our Lord refers to himself as the Good Shepherd (John 10:11, 14). He is concerned for the sheep (10:13). A good shepherd will sacrifice his own life for his sheep (John 10:11). He knows his sheep and is known by them (10:14).

The same word translated "pastor" is used by the Lord when he commissioned Peter to "shepherd My sheep" (John 21:16). You can learn how he accomplished this task by reading his instructions to certain elders, who are also shepherds (pastors). "Therefore, I exhort the elders among you, as your fellow-elder, . . . *shepherd the flock* of God among you, not under compulsion but voluntarily, according to the will of God; and not for sordid gain, but with eagerness; not yet as lording it over those allotted to your charge, but proving to be examples to the flock" (1 Peter 5:1–3).

In his farewell message, Paul exhorted the Ephesian elders to protect the sheep from false teaching. "Be on guard for yourselves and for all the flock, among which the Holy Spirit has made you overseers, to shepherd the church of God which He purchased with with His own blood. I know that after my departure savage wolves will come in among you, not sparing the flock; and from among your own selves men will arise, speaking perverse things, to draw away the disciples after them. Therefore be on the alert, remembering that night and day for a period of three years I did not cease to admonish each one with tears" (Acts 20:28–31).

These passages give excellent information about a shepherding ministry. In summary, the person who is gifted as a pastor-teacher will feed, strengthen, heal, bind up, bring back, seek, lead, protect, sacrifice himself, and demonstrate concern for his flock of spiritual sheep. He will know them personally and they will know him. He will minister because he wants to. He will serve with eagerness as a spiritual example to the flock.

questions

1. Does *every pastor* also have the gift of teaching?

I don't believe every pastor has the gift of teaching. Nor do I believe that every teacher has the gift of pastor. The office of pastor and the office of teacher don't guarantee the gift of pastor-teacher. However, though the gift of teaching doesn't guarantee the gift of pastor, the gift of pastor, because of its function, must include the gift of teaching. How can one feed the sheep if he can't teach? In fact, if you look at the qualifications of an elder, you'll see that teaching is an essential part of pastoring (1 Timothy 3:2)

2. How does the pastor-teacher gift differ from the *gift of evangelism?*

The pastor-teacher works with the evangelist as the pediatrician works with the obstetrician. Billy Graham often refers to himself as a spiritual obstetrician who brings the child into the world. Once the child is born he is placed under the care of the pediatrician for proper growth. That's the responsibility of the pastor-teacher.

3. How can this gift be used *outside the office of pastor-teacher?*

Sunday school teachers, youth sponsors, and children's church workers may be using this gift. Some may just teach. Others will shepherd as they teach. Those teachers and workers who go beyond the scheduled program by pouring their lives into their students will carry on a shepherding ministry.

Others use this gift as counselors or deans in schools. One friend of mine is responsible for student placement in a Christian college, yet is so gifted as a pastor-teacher that students look to him as their spiritual father.

Joan spends a lot of time conducting Bible studies. She uses the Scriptures to encourage, counsel, and exhort other women from the Word of God. She sacrifices her time and finances to visit and build up believers in Christ. She takes the initiative in inviting people. Systematically she invites friends and neighbors to her home. And what begins as a purely get-acquainted evening may end up as a home Bible study.

One of Joan's greatest attractions is that she uses the pastor-teacher gift for her family. Some equally gifted women fall into the trap of teaching others from house to house while they neglect their families. But Joan realizes that what is good for others can also benefit her own family. Ask anyone in her church. Her family is a prime example of a beautiful Christian home.

One word of caution if you think this is your gift. Don't assume that you are God's gift to everyone. Just as a new pastor may lose some of his members to another church because they don't want to follow him, so you also may lose some people. Personalities clash. Certain ideas are too different to work together. Some sheep don't want a shepherd; they want to be on their own.

But stay clear of jealousy. Plenty of people need you. You won't have to steal another's followers. Take care of those who come to you.

make it clear

The teacher who made the greatest impression on me during college was Dr. Charles C. Ryrie, then president and professor at the Philadelphia College of Bible. He influenced my life both by his availability and his teaching.

Dr. Ryrie's teaching is built on the philosophy, "The man who says it most simply, knows it best." Anybody can make the simple difficult, but it takes a gifted teacher to make the difficult understandable.

If you read any of Dr. Ryrie's books or hear him speak, you'll see that he practices what he preaches. He has the gift of making it clear.

THE GIFT OF TEACHING

The gift of evangelism brings new life. The gift of teaching sustains life. Without teaching there can be no discipleship (Matthew 28:19, 20). Ignore teaching and you eliminate spiritual maturity (Colossians 1:28). In fact, lack of teaching has been the dilemma of many churches.

Jim Franklin comes to Christ. A counselor tells him he now possesses eternal life. His sins are forgiven. If he ever needs help, God will sustain him. With this kernel of biblical insight, Jim is on his own to live the Christian life. When he attends church the preacher says, "Believe and be saved." Jim attends the adult Sunday school class and learns that Paul made three missionary journeys. He also picks up some Sunday school reruns he heard as a child.

Jim becomes frustrated. "Is this all there is to the Christian life? Do I just hold on until I die and go to heaven? Doesn't God have anything to tell me about life right now? I have financial problems. My kids are in those rebellious years. My employer was outraged when he heard I wouldn't go to the office Christmas party. But all I get is more Bible facts about Joshua fighting the battle of Jericho. God, what do you have for me now?"

teaching—a way of life

I empathize with Jim Franklin. I invited Christ into my life when I was nine. But ten years passed before I knew what to do with the sins that accumulated over the years. And I received that information from a neighbor. "Mrs. Weaver," I ventured, "I know I'm a Christian, but I also know that I've sinned since I accepted the Lord into my life. What do I do with those sins? Does God forgive them?" Mrs. Weaver went into the house and brought out her well used Bible. "Ricky, read this verse to me." I read, "If we confess our sins, he is faithful and just to forgive us our sins, and to cleanse us from all unrighteousness" (1 John 1:9, KJV). "But what does it mean to confess?" I asked. "It means you tell Jesus what you've done and ask him to forgive you. He will. He's forgiven me many times."

A teacher? No, not in the professional sense. Mrs. Weaver wasn't a well educated woman. Not by way of gift. She was just a great Christian neighbor who was able to "cause me to learn" something I'd never known before. And that's what teaching is: "Causing people to learn."

Perhaps Paul meant this when he encouraged Titus to instruct older women to teach (Titus 2:3–5). You don't need the gift of teaching to teach people to love. You don't need the gift to teach basic truths of the Word. Paul encouraged all the believers at

Colosse like this: "Let the word of Christ richly dwell within you, with all wisdom teaching and admonishing one another with psalms and hymns and spiritual songs, singing with thankfulness in your hearts to God" (Colossians 3:16).

Had Jim Franklin a neighbor to whom he could turn, he wouldn't be so frustrated. If the members of Jim's church ever taught and admonished one another, many of his needs would be met. But people seem to think that teaching must take place in the classroom through an instructor.

On the other hand, some churches go to the other extreme. They don't consider the gift of teaching when they enlist Sunday school teachers. The only qualifications necessary are that the teacher is born again and willing to teach. The result is bored students, frustrated teachers, and a high turnover of Sunday school superintendents. Therefore it's essential to understand what the gift of teaching includes.

teaching—a gift

The gift of teaching is listed third in the biblical order (1 Corinthians 12:28). Teaching began immediately after men came into personal relationship with Jesus. "So then, those who had received his word were baptized; and there were added that day about three thousand souls. And they were continually devoting themselves to *the apostles' teaching* and to fellowship, to the breaking of bread and to prayer" (Acts 2:41, 42). Formal teaching was under the direction of those who had the gift—the apostles.

God saw to it that there would be enough teachers to build up the body of Christ. He gave Paul the gift (2 Timothy 1:11). Barnabas, who possessed the gift of exhortation, also had the gift of teaching (Acts 15:35). Apollos is listed among the teachers (Acts 18:24, 25). And one of the qualifications of an elder is that he be "able to teach" (1 Timothy 3:2).

But what is this gift? If teaching is "causing people to learn," there must first be communication. Something must be communicated. The gift of teaching must be the ability to acquire and communicate truth so effectively that people are caused to learn.

acquiring truth

Acquiring truth begins with analysis, that is, the breaking down of the whole. The gifted teacher takes the complete Bible in hand and chooses a certain portion for study. He investigates the passage by asking questions. Who is speaking? What is he saying? Why does he use this particular word? What does the writer mean? But the teacher doesn't stop with observation. He isn't satisfied with just knowing what the writer has said. He wants to see this truth applied to life. What is the passage saying to me? What does it say to those I am teaching?

After he analyzes the passage, the gifted teacher puts it all back together. He selects the best of his discovery. He wants to be certain that his pupils are exposed to what they are capable of handling. Some of his "nuggets" will have to be placed on a back burner. His students aren't ready for those truths now.

Once the teacher selects the important truths for his particular students, he begins to systematize his findings. He decides what should be given first. He arranges his material logically.

communicating truth

Now he's ready to communicate. He may lecture. He may discuss. He may use visual aids. Perhaps a tape recorder or a filmstrip will be helpful. The pupils participate. They may play the roles in the story. The teacher helps them see how this ancient truth is practical for their lives today. When the pupils learn, the teacher has taught.

When Jesus taught Nicodemus about the new birth, Nicodemus asked two questions: "How can a man be born when he is old? How can these things be?" (John 3:4, 9). The rest of the time Jesus "lectured." Later, with the woman at the well, his approach was indirect. There was dialogue, give-and-take. When she first approached the well he didn't say, "Woman, you must be born again." He said, "Give Me a drink" (John 4:7). That was all he needed to say for the conversation to progress to spiritual truths.

The Apostle Paul taught Jews and Gentiles, Greek philosophers, King Agrippa, the Ephesian elders. Sometimes he spoke as an authoritarian (Acts 13:16–41). At times he used rhetorical questions (Galatians 3:1–5). At times he was tender (Acts 20:17–35). At other times he was harsh (Acts 23:1–3).

The teacher as a communicator realizes that his method and manner of presentation must coincide with his pupils' needs and temperaments.

areas of confusion

Why is it that people learn so little at church? The reasons are legion. However, many churches make three common mistakes in selecting teachers.

1. They select *school teachers* to teach in Sunday school. This confuses the gift with the profession. I thank God for every school teacher who is motivated to help students learn some area of truth, but not all school teachers possess the gift of teaching.

2. A second area of confusion is to think that *a good student* is necessarily a good teacher. How often have you sat in an adult class taught by Dr. Jones from the university? He is a professor by occupation. He was an excellent student. He is a leader in his field. But in Sunday school he's a bore. He analyzes, systematizes, and scrutinizes the minutest details. He finds problems that no other person knew existed and about which no one cares. He raises and answers questions that are totally irrelevant to the needs of his Sunday school class. As Dr. Howard Hendricks puts it, "He scratches where no one itches."

3. The third common mistake churches make when they enlist teachers is to *equate availability with capability*. The way *not* to find qualified teachers is to ask publicly for volunteer help. Some Christians feel that it's spiritual to volunteer for service, even if they're unqualified. I agree that at times a job must be done, and if those who are capable are unavailable, then a less capable person may have to tackle it. But this should be the exception.

women and teaching

It's obvious that many women are wonderfully gifted with teaching. And yet the Bible seems to place limitations on women teaching in the church. Paul wrote to Timothy, "But I do not allow a woman to teach or exercise authority over a man, but to remain quiet" (1 Timothy 2:12). A parallel passage to the Corinthians warns, "Let the women keep silent in the churches; for they are not permitted to speak, but let them subject themselves, just as the Law also says. And if they desire to learn anything, let them ask their own husbands at home; for it is improper for a woman to speak in church" (1 Corinthians 14:34, 35).

Is Paul saying that even though a woman is gifted, she may not use her gift in church? Let's look at the two passages. They have several ideas in common. Both passages are speaking about public worship. And they both prohibit women to "exercise authority over men." The phrase "exercise authority" literally means "to lord it over" someone.

In *The Pastoral Epistles* Dr. Homer Kent comments on 1 Timothy 2:12. "This has reference solely to the function of the authoritative teacher of doctrine in the church . . . The teacher was the declarer of doctrine. Another name for 'teacher' was 'rabbi' (John 1:38)."[1]

The woman, though not inferior mentally, morally, or spiritually to man, is nevertheless subject to him. Paul says that God first created Adam and then made Eve from Adam (1 Timothy 2:13). The divine purpose was for woman to be man's helper, not a dictator over him. A second reason for her subjection is that Eve attempted to lead Adam rather than follow him. The result was deception and sin (1 Timothy 2:14). God told Adam, "Don't eat of this tree." But the serpent told Eve, "Go ahead. Try it. You'll like it." Instead of remaining in submission to what her husband taught her, she disobeyed God's restriction. By her action she challenged God's declaration that the fruit would be harmful.

Dr. William Hendriksen paraphrases Paul's intention like this: "Let a woman not enter a sphere of activity for which by dint of her creation she is not suited. Let not a bird try to dwell under water. Let not a fish try to live on land. Let not a woman yearn

1 Homer Kent, *The Pastoral Epistles* (Chicago: Moody Press, 1958), pp. 112, 113.

to exercise authority over a man by lecturing him in public worship."[2]

This doesn't prohibit women from teaching other women or children. Paul himself wrote, "Older women . . . teaching what is good, that they may encourage the young women to love their husbands, to love their children" (Titus 2:3, 4). Paul told Timothy, "You, however, continue in the things you have learned and become convinced of, knowing from whom you have learned them and that *from childhood* you have known the sacred writings" (2 Timothy 3:14, 15a). Timothy's early instruction came from his grandmother, Lois, and his mother, Eunice (2 Timothy 1:5).

A woman along with her husband may at times teach a man the Scriptures. According to Acts 18:26 both Priscilla and Aquila took Apollos aside after hearing him preach. He was a good preacher but he hadn't finished his theology course. He was only acquainted with the baptism of John. So this husband-and-wife team led him deeper into the ways of God. In this situation, Priscilla wasn't usurping her husband's authority. She was a teaching helpmate.

But what about the woman missionary? She goes out to the field, but where are the Christian men? Dare she try to win the nationals to Christ, and then teach them the Scriptures? Dr. Charles Ryrie answers this question: "There are many times on both the home and foreign fields when there are simply no men to do the work. In such instances this writer feels that we need to remember that Paul not only commanded that things be done decently and in order but also that they be done. In such cases, then, one feels that it is better to do the work with qualified women—even though this is not the ideal—than to sit back and do nothing simply because there are no men. However, women must be cautioned against continuing in such work after there are trained men available for the job. Any woman who finds herself doing a man's work should so aim her own work that a man can

2 William Hendriksen, *New Testament Commentary: 1 & 2 Timothy & Titus* (Grand Rapids: Baker Book House, 1957), p. 109.

assume it as quickly as possible. The acid test any woman can apply to such situations is simply this: Would I be willing to give over all my work to a trained man if he should appear today?"[3]

In summary, I would suggest that women use their gift of teaching with women and children in public gatherings. They stand on scriptural ground to apply their gift here. Home Bible studies, share groups, vacation Bible school, and Sunday school provide significant opportunities for women to use their God-given ability.

The gift of teaching is foundational for any local church. Without it the church crumbles. If your local church has no gifted teacher, follow Jesus's exhortation. Pray the Lord of the harvest to send forth laborers. Ask God to awaken this gift in one of your members, or send you someone who has the gift.

You may be wondering if you have this gift. Why not take a teacher-training course? If your church doesn't have one, find a class at another church. Ask if they'd mind your sitting in on their sessions. Then go back to your own church and apply some of the principles. Another valuable asset is V.B.S. training. When publishing companies send their respresentatives to large churches in your city, take advantage of that training. You may not plan to teach V.B.S., but the training will help you in Sunday school or any other teaching situation. You'll be thrilled to see the gradual change in your pupils' attitudes, understanding, and character, as you faithfully teach them God's Word.

3 Charles Ryrie, *The Role of Women in the Church* (Chicago: Moody Press, 1968), p. 80.

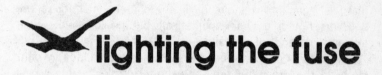

lighting the fuse

"I'm telling you for the last time. Shape up or ship out! You're not prepared when you come to class. Your kids are bored. And I'm getting tired of complaining parents. You've got one more chance, so don't blow it!"

That's one Sunday school superintendent's concept of the gift of exhortation. And I wouldn't be surprised if there are others who think that exhortation means giving someone a piece of their mind.

The word *exhortation* is derived from two Greek words, *para* (alongside) and *Kaleo* (to call). You may be familiar with the term *paraclete*. Jesus calls the Holy Spirit a paraclete (comforter: one who is called to aid or to support another). The gift of exhortation is the ability to help another by motivating him to action. The exhorter lights the fuse.

THE GIFT OF EXHORTATION

The Apostles used the gift of exhortation *to challenge* men to take action. Paul challenged Christians to place our bodies at God's disposal as a living and holy sacrifice (Romans 12:1). He challenged the Corinthians to fulfill the financial pledge they made the previous year (2 Corinthians 9:5). Jude challenged his readers to contend for the faith (Jude 3). In each case the word *exhort* (*parakaleo*) is used. In the first reference, Paul appealed on the basis of God's mercies. When he wrote to the Corinthians his argument was based on the integrity of their spiritual life. Paul hadn't forced them to help the impoverished Christians in Jerusalem: they had volunteered, they had given their word. And so Paul appealed to their integrity. "Is your spiritual life being choked by coveteousness or is there some other reason for the delay?" When Jude challenged his readers to contend for the faith, he warned that false teaching was already in the church. Therefore those believers shouldn't sit back apathetically but should take the initiative and contend for the faith.

Suppose a man has been living a self-centered life for years. He hears the Word of God. The exhorter challenges him to get out of the driver's seat of his life. "Let Jesus take control. You're experiencing frustration and emptiness because you want life to be one grand ego trip. You've done things your way, but where have you gone? Jesus knows what is best. He can supply your needs and desires. Tell him he can have you as you are. Trust him to do what he promised when he said, 'I am come that they might have life and have it more abundantly.'"

The man responds by quietly praying in his heart, "Lord, that man's talking about me. I have been selfish. I haven't given you a chance to run my life. I've messed up myself and my family. Please take me as I am and do something good with me. I can't."

It's exciting to witness the change that takes place when a person responds to exhortation. His family is amazed. And the exhorter is humbled to realize that God has used his gift to change a life.

But exhortation isn't limited to a public challenge. Some people never get a chance to use their gift publicly; they are never in a leadership position. Their gift is used in a more private and quiet way. For instance, *encouragement* is a vital part of exhortation. Notice how Paul tells a group of believers to receive a backslidden brother: "Sufficient for such a one is this punishment which was inflicted by the majority, so that on the contrary you should rather forgive and comfort (*parakaleo*) him, lest somehow such a one be overwhelmed by excessive sorrow. Wherefore, I urge you to reaffirm your love for him'' (2 Corinthians 2:6–8).

This man had sinned. His specific transgression was common information. It demanded church discipline. The chastening was effective. But rather than receive the repentant one into fellowship, the church continued to punish him. Paul stated that this brother now needed acceptance and love. The congregation should publicly forgive him. They should encourage him in his Christian growth.

Pastors, marriage counselors, psychologists, psychiatrists, social workers, and other professionals may have this gift. It is sometimes referred to as the gift of counseling. The counselor, professional or layman, doesn't sit in judgment upon his counselee. He doesn't condemn. He listens. He analyzes. He realizes but for the grace of God he could be in the same predicament. He helps the counselee understand the problem. Somewhere in the process he helps the individual see God's attitude towards the problem. His long-range objective will be to help the individual develop confidence in the Lord. He encourages him to turn to the Scriptures in time of need. And he keeps his door open for return visits if necessary.

The exhorter may use his gift in a third way, as a *rebuke*. When improper behavior exists, reprimand is essential. Look at the Philippian church, an admirable group of Christians. They were united in spirit and purpose. They gave liberally to Paul's financial support. They prayed for his safety and success in preaching the gospel. But two of their congregation were causing disturbance. The dissenters apparently were influential women who weren't getting along with one another. Paul had to rebuke them: ''I urge (*parakaleo*) Euodia and I urge Syntyche to live in harmony in the Lord'' (Philippians 4:2). Peter rebuked Ananias and Sapphira for lying to the Apostles and the Holy Spirit (Acts 5:1–11). Paul rebuked Peter (Cephas) publicly because he played the role of a hypocrite at a banquet. He had quietly left the Gentiles and sat with the Jews when he saw several Jewish elders arrive (Galatians 2:11–14).

It would be beautiful if all Christians were mature. But so

many behave like children; they scream, have temper tantrums, and complain when things don't go their way. They refuse to share their position with another: "Once a member of the church board, always a member." They make mountains out of mole hills. They want to be coddled. If the preacher doesn't give them continuous attention, he isn't a real pastor. If people don't always tell them how much they're missed when absent, the church has become unfriendly.

"Foolishness is bound up in the heart of a child; the rod of discipline will remove it far from him" (Proverbs 22:15). And I believe that there are spoiled believers in churches today because exhorters have refused to rebuke childish behavior. Rebuke isn't "telling someone off" or "giving him a piece of your mind." The purpose of rebuke is to correct improper behavior, not to vent your emotions. Rebuke can take the form of a plea, as when Paul pleaded with Euodia and Syntyche. At times it may include face-to-face encounter with a man. You state his problem and tell him what you think could be done about it. But make certain that you reprimand only when someone's behavior is inconsistent with Scripture. Don't rebuke because it's different from your personal standard. Paul didn't rebuke Peter because he had a beard. He confronted him because he had discriminated against the Gentiles.

To summarize the uses of this gift, consider the case of a man living immorally with a woman. The exhorter *rebukes* the man for his conduct. Not only do the Scriptures condemn his action, but his own conscience condemns him. The man has felt guilty, even though he has probably told himself that love makes it all right. The exhorter then *challenges* the man to change his way of life. "Flee immorality" (1 Corinthians 6:18). "Break off your relationship with this woman." "You are sinning against your own body" (1 Corinthians 6:18). "God wants you to be pure" (1 Thessalonians 4:3–8). "The thief sins alone, but the adulterer causes another to sin."

If the individual repents of his sin and seeks God's forgiveness, the need to rebuke has ended. There is no need to challenge him to turn to Christ. The exhorter now accepts and encourages him.

so you want to exhort

Rebuke, challenge, and encouragement are the major ways by which the exhorter can motivate people to action. Yet two other ingredients are necessary, patience and instruction. Paul instructed Pastor Timothy, "Exhort, with great patience and instruction" (2 Timothy 4:2). Some respond almost immediately; others ignore you. They try your patience. They refuse your advice. And when they fall on their faces you'll be tempted to say, "I told you so." But if you're to be a good exhorter, you need an ocean of patience.

Your other necessity is knowledge of the Word. Timothy was to exhort with instruction. The nondirective approach to counseling has its place. Obviously you must permit the counselee to talk. He needs to express himself. You'll understand him better when you hear how he sees the problem. But more is needed than "uh huh," "I see," "That makes sense," "And then what happened?" There must be instruction. And when you instruct you'll either instruct with human wisdom or divine revelation. You'll use what you know best. Therefore saturate yourself with a working knowledge of God's truth.

exhortation and other gifts

Exhortation and prophecy are related. John the Baptist was a prophet. And as prophet he *challenged* Israel: "Repent, for the kingdom of heaven is at hand" (Matthew 3:2). Peter fulfilled his prophetic role by *rebuking* Israel: "But you disowned the Holy and Righteous One, and asked for a murderer to be granted to you, but put to death the Prince of Life" (Acts 3:14, 15a). The prophet had the companion gift of exhortation. "But one who prophesies speaks to men for edification and *exhortation* and consolation" (1 Corinthians 14:3) "For you can all prophesy one by one, so that all may learn and all may be exhorted" (1 Corinthians 14:31). Similarities exist between exhortation and prophecy, but also differences.

The original gift of prophecy included foretelling. But the gift of exhortation doesn't include predicting future events. In addition, the exhorter is primarily a motivator. Whether he rebukes, encourages, or challenges, his primary aim is to dislodge the complacent and redirect the wayward.

Further, the prophet deals with topics related to life. He may proclaim praises to God, as David recorded in the Psalms. He may talk of God's grace. He may speak of the beauty of the Lord in his holiness. He isn't asking for a decision or a commitment. He is primarily concerned with telling people about God. But the exhorter is basically problem-oriented. He seeks to produce a change. He aims for decision. Joshua was a prime example of an exhorter when he appealed to Israel, "Choose for yourselves today whom you will serve . . . but as for me and my house, we will serve the Lord" (Joshua 24:15).

The gift of mercy often accompanies the gift of exhortation. Without mercy a man will tend to condemn or prejudge those with troubles. But rather than condemn, the exhorter listens and encourages.

The gift of evangelism most likely includes the gift of exhortation. The preacher may be able to proclaim the gospel clearly, the people hear him ask for a decision, but few respond. In contrast the evangelist says the same thing as the preacher, but when he extends the invitation people come. They are motivated to make a decision.

I heard Dr. Malcolm Cronk describe an experience he had with this gift. In his first year as pastor of the Church of the Open Door, Los Angeles, his preaching seemed effective. The people were blessed. Growth was already visible. But few individuals were publicly coming to Christ. Dr. Cronk preached Christ, but when he extended the invitation the people remained in their seats.

Then one of his staff members made a request. "Dr. Cronk, I believe God has given me the gift of exhortation. Would it be possible that after you've preached, I give the invitation?" Dr. Cronk hesitated at first. But then he decided to let his staff worker try the experiment.

The people gathered for the service as they did other Sundays. Familiar hymns filled the sanctuary. Dr. Cronk expounded the Scriptures. The Word of God penetrated hearts prepared by the Holy Spirit. Then the message stopped. Dr. Cronk stepped back. The staff worker came to the pulpit and began his exhortation. Within minutes several individuals left their seats and began their walk to the front of the church. Then others came. And still others.

This procedure wasn't repeated every Sunday. "But there are those times when I sense the leading of the Holy Spirit to turn the remainder of the service over to my staff worker. He exhorts the people to come and make their decision for Christ. They come."

You may wonder how to tell whether you have this gift. One sure way is to ask yourself, "Do people respond when I exhort them?" When Peter rebuked Israel for crucifying Jesus, they cried, "What shall we do?" (Acts 2:37–40). John the Baptist challenged his listeners so much that they trembled, "What shall we do?" (Luke 3:10, 12).

If most people whom you exhort tell you to mind your own business, it may be wise to look at other gifts. But if people respond, your gift may be exhortation.

see it as it is

I know of few places as beautiful as California's San Joaquin Valley in the spring. The citrus, nut, and fruit blossoms fill the landscape with beauty and fragrance. Purples, reds, pinks, and whites cluster in the orchards. The foothills of the Sierras display their beauty with yellow, blue, and brown flowers scattered through the fresh green grass. Acres of vineyards cover the fields. Dozens of palm varieties adorn the streets and add the tropical touch.

But winter is another story. Though there are some warm, clear days, the Valley experiences many cold, foggy days. A rising fog over the fig orchards produces an eerie effect, and at such a time a visitor to this part of California could be greatly disappointed. He would come expecting to see the sunshine, but he might not see it again until he was back on the plane, flying over the high winter fog. He hears about the beautiful snow-capped mountains bordering the entire eastern side of Fresno. They can be so brilliant, that you feel you can reach them at the end of your yard. But when the fog descends, you can't see the end of your yard.

God gave certain gifts to men that help him penetrate the fog of deceit, delusion, and natural inability to "see it as it is." The Holy Spirit provides the gifts of wisdom, knowledge, and discernment.

THE GIFT OF WISDOM

The hour was late. The minds and bodies of fourteen men were straining to keep alert. For the past hour and a half this church board had made little progress. A decision had to be made that night but they had come to a stalemate. The arguments had been given for the two major viewpoints. The votes had been taken three times, but each time they ended with a seven/seven tie.

As the debate continued one of the fourteen asked for the floor. He had listened carefully to both sides of the issue. But the more he listened the less convinced he was that either proposal was good, including the one for which he had voted. Now, hesitantly, he suggested a third alternative.

Faces brightened. His proposal made sense. It was so simple, why hadn't anyone thought of it before? Within minutes it was unanimously adopted.

That incident shows the gift of wisdom in action. This gift is the ability to make God's will known to men. It is the capacity to apply spiritual principles to contemporary problems. The person with this gift asks himself, "What would God want done in this situation?"

biblical examples

One of the first occurrences of this gift is found in Genesis 41. The Pharaoh of Egypt had a dream. The king was frustrated. He called his magicians and wise men to interpret it. They tried, but they were incapable of understanding the message. Then the chief cupbearer told Pharaoh that a young man named Joseph had interpreted the dreams of his cellmates.

Pharaoh immediately called Joseph into his palace and related his dream to the prisoner. Joseph listened intently. When the Egyptian king finished his story, silence gripped the room. Then Joseph slowly stood to his feet and gave the king the interpretation. As Joseph spoke, Pharaoh realized that Joseph's information came from God. "Since God has informed you of all this, there is no one so discerning and wise as you are. You shall be over my house, and according to your command all my people shall do homage; only in the throne I will be greater than you'' (Genesis 41:39, 40).

Another account of this great gift is demonstrated in the Book of 2 Chronicles. David was dead and his son Solomon was now king. As God appeared to the new king one evening, he told him to ask whatever he wanted.

Solomon replied, ''Give me now wisdom and knowledge, that I may go out and come in before this people; for who can rule this great people of Thine? And God said to Solomon, 'Because you had this in mind, and did not ask for riches, wealth, or honor, or the life of those who hate you, nor have you asked for long life, and you have asked for yourself wisdom and knowledge, that you may rule my people, over whom I have made you king, wisdom and knowledge have been granted to you' (2 Chronicles 1:11, 12).

Solomon was gifted with both wisdom and knowledge. He used these gifts throughout his reign. For instance, one time two women brought a baby to him. Each claimed to be its mother. Solomon solved the problem with great wisdom: ''Divide the living child in two, and give half to the one and half to the other'' (1 Kings 3:25). Of course, the one woman pleaded for the life of the child. When Solomon heard the plea he replied, ''Give the first woman the living child, and by no means kill him. She is the mother'' (1 Kings 3:27). The news of Solomon's wisdom spread throughout all Israel and then into other regions.

When the Queen of Sheba heard about Solomon's wisdom, she came to his kingdom to ask him many difficult questions. After days of conversation and observation, she said, ''It is a true report which I heard in my own land about your words and your wisdom. Nevertheless I did not believe the reports, until I came and my eyes had seen it. And behold, the half was not told me. You exceed in wisdom and prosperity the report which I heard. How blessed are your men. How blessed are these your servants who stand before you continually and hear your wisdom'' (1 Kings 10:6–8).

When Daniel sought God for the interpretation of King Nebuchadnezzar's dream he prayed, ''To Thee, O God of my fathers, I give thanks and praise. For Thou has given me wisdom and power; even now Thou hast made known to me what we requested of Thee. For Thou hast made known to us the king's matter" (Daniel 2:23).

In the New Testament it becomes obvious that all the first deacons were gifted with wisdom. A practical problem arose. The Greek-speaking Jews were complaining that their widows weren't given enough to eat. Wisdom was needed to solve the problem of neglect. The apostles challenged that local assembly of believers like this: "But select from among you, brethren, seven men of good reputation, full of the Spirit and of wisdom, whom we may put in charge of this task" (Acts 6:3).

One of the seven deacons was Stephen. This man not only took care of distributing food, but he also preached (Acts 6:9). And the more he preached the more some people argued with him. "And yet they were unable to cope with the wisdom and the Spirit with which he was speaking" (Acts 6:10). Stephen made sense. They didn't like what he said, but he made sense.

the gift and general wisdom

But how does the gift of wisdom differ from other forms of wisdom? The Scriptures speak of three types of general wisdom.

1. There is the *natural wisdom* of man that flows from his inherited intellectual capacity which, coupled with the sum of his lived experiences, enables him to capably analyze various problems. This wisdom is not "worldly" in the sense that it opposes God. It is rather the fruit of the intellectual reasoning process that provides the best answers to man's problems. Those who have such wisdom neither recognize God as its source nor rely on him for its development.

This wisdom is illustrated in the Book of Acts where the town clerk of Ephesus used natural wisdom to spare the lives of Gaius and Aristarchus, Paul's traveling companions from Macedonia (Acts 19:29, 35–41). It may be used extensively by lawyers, doctors, politicians, and others.

2. Another type of general wisdom is the *"worldly" wisdom* against which God has declared war. "For it is written, I will destroy the wisdom of the wise, and the cleverness of the clever I will set aside. Where is the wise man? Where is the scribe?

Where is the debater of this age? Has not God made foolish the wisdom of the world? For since in the wisdom of God the world through its wisdom did not come to know God, God was well pleased through the foolishness of the message preached to save those who believe'' (1 Corinthians 1: 19–21). The wisdom of the natural man is in direct opposition to God's wisdom. It is the wisdom that causes men to conclude that God didn't create the universe (Genesis 1:1, 2). It's the wisdom that proclaims there are many ways to God (John 14:6; Acts 4:12; Proverbs 14:12). It's the wisdom that keeps man from placing his trust in God (1 Corinthians 1:21). Its the wisdom that James describes as ''. . . earthly, natural, demonic'' (James 3:15).

3. There is also a third type of general wisdom. It is *available to every believer* who asks God for his wisdom in a particular circumstance. ''But if any of you lacks wisdom, let him ask God, who gives to all men generously and without reproach, and it will be given to him'' (James 1:5). James further describes this wisdom as ''. . . first pure, then peaceable, gentle, reasonable, full of mercy and good fruits, unwavering, without hypocrisy'' (James 3:17). Pastors constantly look to God for this wisdom during counseling sessions. Young people may use this wisdom in choosing their life mate or occupation. Parents should avail themselves of this wisdom as they seek to rear their children in the way of the Lord.

In contrast to this general wisdom is the gift of wisdom. The gift will differ in content from the first two types of general wisdom. The gift of wisdom is *biblically oriented*. It is consistent with the will of God. It is the *logos* (word) of wisdom. It applies God's truth to contemporary problems. It never counsels a person to do anything contrary to God's will. Christian psychologists, marriage counselors, pastors, and laymen who have this gift won't tell their counselees to take a course of action inconsistent with God's will.

This gift of wisdom differs from the first two types of general wisdom in a second way. When this gift was used in the Scriptures it *produced a reaction that caused men to consider God.* Pharaoh replied to Joseph, ''Since God has informed you of this . . .'' (Genesis 41:39). When Solomon made his pronouncement about what should be done with the child brought before him, the people ''saw that the wisdom of God was in him'' (1 Kings 3:28).

The Queen of Sheba replied to Solomon, "Blessed be the Lord your God who delighted in you to set you on the throne of Israel" (1 Kings 10:9). After he was told the interpretation of his dreams, King Nebuchadnezzar replied to Daniel, "Surely your God is a God of gods and a Lord of kings and a revealer of mysteries, since you have been able to reveal this mystery" (Daniel 2:47).

In the New Testament, when the deacons used the gift of wisdom, the Bible records, "And the word of God kept on spreading; and the numbers of the disciples continued to increase greatly in Jerusalem and a great many of the priests were becoming obedient to the faith" (Acts 6:7). And though it was an adverse effect, Stephen's wisdom produced a reaction that caused men to consider God. "You men who are stiff-necked and uncircumcised in heart and ears are always resisting the Holy Spirit; you are doing just as your fathers did" (Acts 7:51).

But how does the gift differ from the general wisdom available to all believers? Primarily *in the consistency of use and results.* The individual gifted with wisdom will consistently make wise decisions and provide godly insights for problems. The results will be pure, peaceable, gentle, reasonable, full of mercy and good fruits, unwavering and without hypocrisy.

The person using this gift will soon become known among his associates. He will be the one individuals consult as they face problems. He will be the opinion setter in the church whether he holds an office or not. His opinion will be highly respected.

If you possess and use this gift, people won't always agree with you, although some will praise God for your wise counsel. But because all of us still possess the old nature, your wisdom may infuriate others. They may suspect you're right. They may in their hearts agree that what you suggest is best. They may be aware that what you say is God's will. But your proposal may demand a change of attitude. It may ask for control on strong desires. Therefore, people may become irritated with you. True, they will be forced to face the will of God, but they may not accept it.

If the gift of wisdom is yours, use it to build up believers. So many Christians need good counsel. They have problems that seem insurmountable. Churches grope in the dark as they attempt to figure out why they aren't growing. Your gift may be the catalyst God wants to use to do a great work. Of course, one of the major evidences that you have this gift is that the Holy Spirit will give you a humble spirit in using your gift. This characteristic in your life will result in God being glorified rather than you, when others see your gift of wisdom in operation.

THE GIFT OF KNOWLEDGE

Does a high IQ guarantee that you possess the gift of knowledge? No, Intelligence Quotient has little to do with that gift.

When I first studied the gift of knowledge I understood it as the ability to understand, analyze, and interpret the Word of God to others. But this description fits the gift of teaching (chapter 6) better. Investigating further, I now believe that the gift of knowledge is the ability to understand truth that is unknown by natural means.

old testament illustrations

Two Old Testament men who demonstrated the gift of knowledge were the prophets Nathan and Elisha. David, king of Israel, had sinned by taking another man's wife. He hoped to conceal his act by sending the woman's husband to the front lines to be killed in battle.

As David sat in his palace, Nathan came to him and told a story. There was a rich man and a poor man in a city. The rich man had many flocks and herds, but the poor man had only one small lamb. It became his pet. He and his family loved it. It was like a member of the family.

A traveler stopped by the rich man's house. The wealthy host wanted to be hospitable, but without paying any price. So he butchered the poor man's pet lamb and served it to the traveler.

David was furious: "As the Lord lives, surely the man who has done this deserves to die. And he must make restitution for the lamb fourfold, because he did this thing and had no compassion." But then Nathan looked at David and said, "You are the man!" (2 Samuel 12:1–14).

How did Nathan know about David's sin? Through the palace grapevine? Did Bathsheba spread the news to her friends? No, Nathan received his information from God (2 Samuel 12:1). This sin couldn't go unjudged. It couldn't be swept under the rug. A woman had become unfaithful to her husband, and now he had been killed, according to David's devilish plan. The gift of knowledge exposed that sin.

This gift was used by the prophet Elisha when he exposed the sin of his servant, Gehazi (2 Kings 5:20–27). It was again used by Elisha when the king of Syria was at war with Israel. The king of Syria determined a specific place for an attack on Israel, but when the Syrians arrived at the designated spot, Israel was waiting for them. The king regrouped his men and made another plan of attack. But again Israel was waiting for him. After this happened several times, the Syrian king called a high-level strategy meeting. "Will you tell me which of us is for the king of Israel?" he raged. "There must be a traitor among us. It's impossible for the enemy to know our every move."

No one responded. They feared for their lives. Then a servant replied, "No, my Lord, O King; but Elisha, the prophet who is in Israel, tells the king of Israel the words that you speak in your bedroom" (2 Kings 6:8–14). How about that! Every time the Syrian king spoke in secret, Elisha was tuned in to the secret by the Spirit of God. He had the gift of knowledge.

other illustrations

Peter used his gift of knowledge on at least two occasions. When Jesus asked about others' opinions of his identity, his disciples reported, "Some say John the Baptist; some, Elijah; and others, Jeremiah, or one of the prophets" (Matthew 16:14). Then Jesus focused his question on them. "But who do you say that I am?" "Thou art the Christ, the Son of the living God," Peter answered.

How did he know that? Jesus saves us any guesswork about the source. "Blessed are you, Simon Barjona, because flesh and blood did not reveal this to you, but My Father who is in heaven"

(Matthew 16:17). Peter had information that came completely outside of himself. It came from God.

The gift of knowledge isn't related to intelligence. It's the ability to grasp the truth about a situation that cannot be known by natural means. Dr. W. A. Criswell tells of an incident involving F. B. Meyer, the famous preacher.[1] As he was preaching in the Free Assembly Hall in Edinburgh he stated, "There is a man here who owes his employer three pounds and eighteen shillings. Until that sum is repaid, that young man will never have peace with God." F. B. Meyer was unaware of whom he was speaking. He was using the gift of knowledge to uncover a hidden sin. But later a young man made an appointment to see him. He asked the preacher if he knew him. "No, I never saw you before." The astonished youth replied, "In your sermon you described exactly what I did. My soul has been troubled ever since. Already there is a letter in the mail with a check returning the money."

Previous to President Kennedy's trip to Dallas, Billy Graham called the White House and told them he felt that something dreadful was going to happen to the President. Mr. Graham asked that President Kennedy postpone his trip. The White House thanked the evangelist for his concern, but the trip was not cancelled.

ESP? Psychic phenomena? Dabbling with demons? No, this is the exercise of the gift of knowledge.

THE GIFT OF DISCERNMENT OF SPIRITS

Every day someone in this country sells good merchandise for worthless currency. The money looks real, it feels like legal tender, but it's counterfeit. It's phony, not worth a dime.

In religion, human philosophies, cults, and sects run rampant. Some are poor counterfeit, but others are carefully recreated masterpieces. Even professing Christians are entrapped in their snare.

Eternity magazine editor, William Petersen, writes, "We are

---

1 W. A. Criswell, *The Holy Spirit in Today's World* (Grand Rapids: Zondervan Publishing House, 1966), p. 141.

completely neglecting newer cults that are making converts among our young people by the thousands . . . America has never seen a time when its young people have been so religious and yet so non-Christian."[2] But the problem of cults isn't new. It's as old as the beginning of Christianity.

In the first century there was no New Testament as we know it. An epistle could be found in one city and a gospel in another. John the Apostle was still writing his five "books" near the close of that century.

The apostles warned that problems would arise in the churches. Paul admonished the elders of Ephesus, "I know that after my departure savage wolves will come in among you, not sparing the flock; and from among your own selves men will arise, speaking perverse things, to draw away the disciples after them" (Acts 20:29, 30). He expressed his fear to the Corinthians that they might be led astray by counterfeit teachers. "For such men are false apostles, deceitful workers, disguising themselves as apostles of Christ. And no wonder, for even Satan disguises himself as an angel of light. Therefore it is not surprising if his servants also disguise themselves as servants of righteousness; whose end shall be according to their deeds" (2 Corinthians 11:13–15).

God has provided a way to deal with the problem of false spirits. He gave some believers a special gift known as the gift of discerning spirits: ". . . and to another the distinguishing of spirits" (1 Corinthians 12:10).

This gift is demonstrated in the Scripture several times. Apparently the gift of discerning spirits belonged to those who also possessed the gift of prophecy. Paul established an orderly way to use the gift of prophecy. When a prophet spoke, he was to submit himself to the other prophets' discerning gift. "And let two or three prophets speak, and let the others pass judgment . . . And the spirit of prophets are subject to prophets" (1 Corinthians 14:29, 32).

But what if in some assemblies of believers no gift of discerning spirits existed?

2 *The Church Around The World* (March 1973).

The apostles set up several guidelines that could apply to any prophecy or teaching. For instance, those who taught that Jesus was a mere spirit and not a man with a human body were disqualified as God's spokesmen (1 John 4:2, 3). Paul told the Corinthians and Galatians that another way to distinguish spirits was to compare the messenger's Jesus, his spirit, and his gospel with what Paul himself had already taught (2 Corinthians 11:4; Galatians 1:6–10). The special gift of discerning spirits was useful when nothing had been spoken or written on the subject which the prophet or teacher was expounding. If any speaker contradicted what already had been taught by the apostles, he spoke falsely.

Paul demonstrated the gift of discerning spirits when he was on his way to a prayer meeting in Philippi. A slave girl was following Paul and crying out, "These men are the bond-servants of the Most High God, who are proclaiming to you the way of salvation" (Acts 16:17). Many preachers would be thankful for a testimony like that.

But the girl met Paul and his party every day and continued to shout, disturbing their meetings. Paul soon recognized that this was not a testimony to the glory of God. He discerned an evil spirit attempting to disrupt the preaching of God's Word.

Once the Apostle realized the source of the problem he turned to the spirit within the girl and shouted, "I command you in the name of Jesus Christ to come out of her" (Acts 16:18). The evil spirit immediately left the girl.

Today we have a tremendous advantage over the early believers. We have the completed Scriptures. We aren't limited to John's general guidelines. Nor are we limited to some of Paul's teachings. We have God's revelation in his written Word.

The writer of the Hebrews stated that any Christian can develop discernment if he knows and uses the Scriptures in his life (Hebrews 5:12–14). But if he doesn't study the Word of God, he will be a prime prospect for the cultist. Well then, if every Christian has the potential to discern, what about the gift?

Is the gift of discerning spirits being given today? Yes. Dr. Walter Martin, for instance, has written many books on the cults of our day. Much of his ministry is spent comparing cultists' teachings with Scripture.

The New Testament gives us the basic ingredients to discern between truth and error. The Holy Spirit (1 John 2:28) and the Word of God (Hebrews 5:14) become mighty weapons in the hands of a believing Christian. So, if you want greater discernment, study the Bible. Place yourself under competent Christian teachers. Compare Scripture with Scripture. Follow the pattern of the Bereans, who "received the word with great eagerness, examining the Scriptures daily, to see whether these things were so" (Acts 17:11).

 the melody lingers on

A lot of churches delight in being innovative. They try new methods of education, new means of evangelistic outreach, new forms of worship. I wonder how we would feel if we could walk into a worship service from King David's time. Listen to the role that music played in Israel's worship. And note in particular the type of instruments they used.

> "Praise the Lord!
> Praise God in His sanctuary . . .
> Praise Him with trumpet sound;
> Praise Him with harp and lyre
> Praise Him with timbrel and dancing;
> Praise Him with stringed instruments and pipe.
> Praise Him with loud cymbals;
> Praise Him with resounding cymbals" (Psalm 150:1, 3–5).

Wouldn't that shake up the troops in our churches some Sunday morning! Trumpet, stringed instruments, timbrel (tambourine), cymbals. How could anyone focus on God with all that racket?

Sometimes we act as if God would be offended if we showed emotion or raised our voices to express his praise. But how would you feel if you gave your child a bike for Christmas and he merely muttered something. You ask, "What did you say?" Again a mumble. You still don't hear, and you wonder, "Doesn't he like it?" Finally he says in a somewhat louder voice, "I said I like it. I don't have to shout, do I?"

What a difference if your child yelled, "Yippie! Gee, thanks, Mom and Dad! Wait 'till my friends see it. I love it. Yahoo!" Would you be disappointed that he showed emotion? Of course not.

THE GIFT OF MUSIC

When the Jews had something to sing and shout about, they opened all the stops. And when it was time to meditate, they closed their mouths and listened to God. "The Lord is in His holy temple. Let all the earth be silent before Him" (Habakkuk 2:20).

When Israel worshiped, there was a time to be silent and a time to sing and shout praises to God. When the people praised the Lord, they were led by those who had the gift of music. David, beyond doubt, was the most important and well-known musician of Israel.

David: the gifted musician

The first indication of David's musical ability is recorded in 1 Samuel 16:16–18. King Saul had disobeyed God. He determined to live and reign as he pleased (1 Samuel 15:19), and God rejected him as Israel's king (1 Samuel 16:1). The prophet Samuel was sent to Jesse in Bethlehem to select a new king from one of Jesse's sons. Samuel interviewed seven of the sons and God systematically rejected each of them. Frustrated, Samuel asked Jesse if he had any more sons. "There remains yet the youngest, and behold, he is tending the sheep" (1 Samuel 16:11). The prophet sent for David. As the young shepherd stood before Samuel, the Lord said, "Arise, anoint him; for this is he" (1 Samuel 16:12).

As Samuel was anointing David to be the future king of Israel, the Spirit of God departed from King Saul and an evil spirit terrorized him. When the king's servants realized what had happened, they advised the king to find a musician to play and soothe his nerves. One young man suggested someone. "Behold, I have seen a son of Jesse the Bethlehemite who is *a skillful musician,* a mighty man of valor, a warrior, one prudent in speech, and a handsome man; and *the Lord is with him.*" So Saul sent messengers to Jesse, and said, "Send me your son David who is with the flock" (1 Samuel 16:18, 19). So David's gift of music brought him to the palace. "A man's gift makes room for him, and brings him before great men" (Proverbs 18:16).

David's gift of music extended beyond playing musical instruments. He was also a lyricist, a writer of Psalms (poems set to music). Samuel refers to David as "the sweet psalmist of Israel" (2 Samuel 23:1). But was this gift from the Holy Spirit? Is there any proof that when David wrote his Psalms, he was led by the Holy Spirit? Yes. Jesus stated that David's Psalms were a product of the Holy Spirit: "David himself *said in the Holy Spirit,* the Lord said to my Lord, sit at my right hand, until I put thine enemies beneath thy feet" (Mark 12:36).

Certainly David's gift of music wasn't given to him the day he walked into Saul's palace. Most likely this gift was given at birth. Dr. Charles C. Ryrie defines a spiritual gift as "an ability given by God either at birth or at the new birth in order to serve him."[1] As David was out in the hills taking care of the sheep, he passed his time practicing on the harp. And his gift was such that he played before a king while still a teen-ager. David also used his gift to write seventy-three of the 150 Psalms, and to appoint choirs for worship (2 Chronicles 7:6).

Another musically gifted man was David's son, Solomon. "Now God gave Solomon wisdom and very great discernment and breadth of mind . . . he was wiser than all men . . . He also spoke 3,000 proverbs, and *his songs were 1,005*" (1 Kings 4:29–32). Two of his songs are recorded in the Book of Psalms (72, 127). But the greatest of all his songs is "The Song of Solomon." The first verse of this book begins, "The Song of Songs, which is

1 From author's class notes, Dallas Theological Seminary, 1962.

Solomon's." Another translation would be "The *best* of the songs." Solomon's great song was chosen by the Spirit to become part of the Old Testament Scriptures.

the extension of this gift

But the gift of music isn't limited to singing, playing, and writing. The Old Testament records six different uses of this gift. First there were the *instrumentalists*—"all who were skillful with musical instruments" (2 Chronicles 34:12). Then the *singers,* Heman, Asaph, and Ethan (1 Chronicles 15:19). David and Asaph are listed as some of the lyricists or *composers* of music (2 Chronicles 29:30). Add to this list the *choir directors* or conductors (Nehemiah 12:46). The gift of music also included *music instructors* (1 Chronicles 15:22). And the sixth use of the gift was *making instruments* (2 Chronicles 7:6; 29:26, 27).

You may wonder why some people are able to use their gift of music more extensively than others. One possible reason is that they develop it more. Further, they may be willing to try new ways to use it. But another factor is important.

Since many believers have more than one spiritual gift, their gifts can interact. For instance, if you have both the gift of music and the gift of prophecy, you may be able to compose lyrics for songs. If you have the gift of music and the gift of teaching, you may be able to teach music. If you have the gift of music and the gift of craftsmanship, you may be able to make instruments. As the various gifts combine in one individual, greater effectiveness is possible.

New Testament use

The gift of music isn't limited to the Old Testament. "When you assemble, each one has a psalm, has a teaching, has a revelation, has a tongue, has an interpretation. Let all things be done for edification" (1 Corinthians 14:26). If a man has a psalm (a song set to music) to share, he will use the gift of music (Colossians 3:16). "Let the word of Christ richly dwell within you, with all wisdom teaching and admonishing one another, with psalms and hymns and spiritual songs singing with thankfulness in your hearts to God'' (Nestle Greek Testament).

contemporary use of the gift

The gift of music can be used in the local church with children's, youth, and adult choirs; soloists; ensembles and orchestras. The gift can also be used to compose. A teen-ager in our Winnipeg church wrote and sang his own songs. We provided various opportunities for him to use his gift; he was encouraged to develop it.

Composition may be the most neglected way in which Christians use this gift. Since the majority of songs in our hymnbooks were written in the 18th, 19th, and early 20th centuries, I encourage anyone who has the gift of music to consider composing and arranging.

Some young men have taken up this challenge and have produced excellent musicals (such as John Walvoord and Don Wyrtzen's, ''What's It All About Anyhow?''). Many Christians have been blessed by the music of John W. Peterson and Ralph Carmichael. The use of this gift in the area of singing offers the Christian community a wide selection, from Johnny Cash to Jerome Hines.

At the time this book is being written, the number-one recording group in Christian music is Andrae Crouch and the Disciples. A magazine article describes the emphasis that Andrae places on the fact that his gift is from God. ''All the Crouch children sang in Sunday school, but it was at this time, age 9, that a piano and the gift of music entered Andrae's life.

'' 'My dad had been preaching up north of L.A., commuting back and forth. They wanted him to preach full-time, so he put a 'fleece' before the Lord. If the Lord wanted him to pastor at that church, he asked God to give me the gift of music. There was no one there to play the piano. I think he chose me because I was always listening to the record player and tryin' to sing. My mother purchased a piano and my father called me over to the church one day and asked, 'If the Lord gave you the gift of music would you use it?' So they set me on the piano bench and I just started playin'. The congregation had songbooks—I'd have to run up the scale to find the key they were singin' in. But I was soon playin' for them, and later started the choir.'

"Andrae's mother recalls that the first song he played was "What a Friend We Have in Jesus"—with two hands. As you watch Andrae perform today, you can appreciate his God-given talent (he's had no formal music instruction). He has perfect pitch, plays complicated rhythms, in any key, all over the keyboard, with eyes open or closed.

" 'What I know—I just picked it up along the way. God just made it in me,' he explains."[2]

the undeveloped gift

The gift of music is perhaps the most underdeveloped or undeveloped gift of all. How often have you been in a church where you've agonized, listening to a soloist who was either ungifted or who had neglected to develop the gift?

Some well-meaning Christians live with the idea that "anything is good enough for God." Others never consider the possibility of taking lessons. They believe that since their singing came very naturally they have no reason to develop the gift. Others, like myself, took lessons for many years, and practiced just enough to get by; therefore our usefulness in music is limited.

Another reason why we don't have better quality music in our churches is that some people get into a choir and plant their roots. To hint that they may not have the gift offends them immediately. Their argument is that they can't do anything else in the church, meaning that they can't teach or don't want to visit. But, they conclude, you can always sing in the choir.

This isn't to say that every church should demand to have a choir like that in a big city congregation. A church should work with what it has. But the goal of each church should be to honor the Lord with the best quality of music it can produce.

2 "They've Got Confidence," *Christian Life* (February 1973).

hey, buddy, God's alive!

It's an old story, but illustrates the point. A farmer sold his mule, Marvin, to a friend. The man took Marvin home. He hitched him to a plow and yelled, "H'yah! Get movin', Marvin!" But Marvin wouldn't budge. The new owner shouted, pleaded, threatened, and cried. But the mule stood firm as Gibraltar.

The friend called the former owner and demanded his money back. "Why that mule ain't worth a dime. I've seen stubborn mules in my day, but he's the stubbornest!" The man came over to his friend's farm. He asked the new owner to explain once again how he tried to persuade Marvin to pull the plow. "I've talked gently to that mule. I've yelled at him. I've begged him. But he just stands there lookin' like an idiot."

The former owner walked back to the barn and returned carrying a two-by-four. He stood in front of Marvin, raised the two-by-four until he practically touched his heels, and then let loose with a resounding WHACK!

Marvin's knees buckled. He went down with a thud. The new owner was furious. "What'd you do that for? You might have killed him!" The man put his arm around his friend and said, "Sam, don't worry. Marvin will be all right in a few minutes. He's a very special mule. You can't just go up to him and tell him to get movin'. First you have to get his attention."

The Bible refers to us as sheep who go wandering off and

109

therefore need shepherds. At times we behave like Marvin, so God uses special means to get our attention.

God has provided three spiritual gifts that are attention-getters. They are often referred to as the sign gifts: miracles, tongues, and interpretation of tongues.

THE GIFT OF MIRACLES

"Water turned into wine . . . men raised from the dead . . . the ability to eat poison and not be harmed . . . to walk across a river 30 feet deep . . ." Present-day miracles? Such claims have been made in Indonesia. And the impression left on the reader of *Like a Mighty Wind* is that these miracles can be duplicated where genuine faith is released.

That God can perform and has performed miracles is not a problem. It's impossible to think about Christianity without considering miracles, because our Lord is a God of miracles. Approximately 31 percent of the verses in Mark's Gospel alone deal with miracles. But is God duplicating such experiences of the first-century church today? Judge for yourself as you trace the gift through Scripture.

the purpose of miracles

The miracles of Scripture are called signs, wonders, and powers. A miracle is a power beyond man's ability. One purpose of miracles was *to display the power of God.* But miracles also *demonstrated the authority of the miracle worker.* God told Moses to stand before Pharaoh and demand that he release Israel. Moses argued, "What if they will not believe me, or listen to what I say? For they may say, 'The Lord has not appeared to you.' " God authenticated Moses . . . "What is that in your hand?" . . . "A staff" . . . "Throw it to the ground" . . . "It became a serpent" . . . "Stretch out your hand and grasp it by its tail . . . And it became a staff in his hand" . . . "*That they may believe* that the Lord, the God of their fathers, the God of Abraham, the God of Isaac, and the God of Jacob, has appeared to you" (Exodus 4:1–5).

Men saw the power of God. Many also accepted miracle-workers as God-sent. "Rabbi, we know that You have come from God as a teacher; for no one can do these signs that You do unless God is with him" (John 3:2). But miracles accomplished a third objective. They *caused men to listen to God's message.* "And the multitudes with one accord were giving attention to what was said by Philip, as they heard and saw the signs which he was performing" (Acts 8:6).

God's power and God's message expanded throughout that first century. The apostles preached. People listened. Why? "God also bearing witness with them, both by signs and wonders and by various miracles and by gifts of the Holy Spirit according to His own will" (Hebrews 2:4).

the history of miracles

But miracles aren't confined to one period of history. The Old Testament highlights such miracle workers as Moses, Elijah, and Elisha.

Moses sent ten plagues upon Egypt (Exodus 7–12). He divided the Red Sea (Exodus 14). He struck a rock and water gushed forth (Exodus 17). Elijah multiplied a bowl of flour and a jar of oil. He breathed life into a widow's dead son (1 Kings 17). He called fire and rain from heaven (1 Kings 18). Elisha asked for a double portion of Elijah's power. With this double portion he too raised someone from the dead (2 Kings 4:26–36). He purified a pot of poisonous stew (2 Kings 4:38–44). He healed Naaman of his leprosy (2 Kings 5). Elisha floated an iron axe head on water (2 Kings 6).

But the close of the Old Testament is followed by 400 years of silence. God stopped speaking to man. If a prophet spoke, he did so on his own (Zechariah 13:2–5). No revelation. No prophets. No miracles. The gift of miracles had come and gone. As Job wrote about earthly possessions, so it was with miracles: "The Lord gave and the Lord has taken away. Blessed be the name of the Lord" (Job 1:21b).

Then one night a star shone over a stable in the Judean village of Bethlehem. The "fullness of time" had come. Once again God was going to speak to man. This time, however, his message would be flawless, for the messenger was his unique Son. Along with the messenger came a power that hadn't been seen for hundreds of years. People said that he spoke with authority, unlike the other teachers of his day, who merely quoted authorities. This man also healed the sick, cast out demons, silenced the wind, walked on water, gave sight to the blind, gave mobility to the paralyzed, and raised the dead.

Those who followed him performed similar supernatural acts. Paul wrote to the Corinthian church and said of himself: "The signs of a true apostle were performed among you with all perseverance, by signs and wonders and miracles" (2 Corinthians 12:12). Sometimes the miracles were used as a punishment for sin (Acts 5:1–11, 13:8–12). Other times they were used to get a hearing for God (Acts 3:1–12). His final message to man came through the Apostle John.

Then God's direct revelation stopped. The miracles likewise stopped. Within a few hundred years Jesus Christ had become imprisoned behind the doors of the church. For the next thousand years little was heard about salvation by grace. But then intellectual ferment, social change, spiritual renewal, and later industrial revolution began to turn the world upside down. New voices were heard: Erasmus, Wycliffe, Tyndale, Luther, Calvin, Zwingli, Gutenberg. Within a few centuries God was once again speaking to man. He wasn't giving new revelations, but he was directing men to translate and distribute his complete revelation to the man on the street and the farm.

Once again his power was felt. And today, as men read God's Word and believe what he says, they see miracles. Whether in the demon-infested country of Haiti or the sophisticated streets of San Francisco, Satanic spirits are expelled. Christian schools, struggling financially, call out to God for a miracle, and money is provided. Some lie on their death beds, Christians pray for their recovery, and in some cases God restores them to health. Perhaps you yourself have had a close call with death or been in a serious accident. You've concluded, "It was a miracle I wasn't killed!"

Perhaps the greatest of all miracles is the one we experience the day we take Jesus into our life. In an instant we are delivered from the kingdom of darkness to the kingdom of light (Acts 26:18). We pass out of death to life (John 5:24). Our sins are forgiven (Colossians 1:13, 14). We have peace with God (Romans 5:1).

historical summary

Miracles have existed from the first day of creation until now, though God has not publicly used miracles in every generation. The first man gifted to perform miracles was Moses, and throughout the history of Israel God raised up other miracle workers. But after Israel returned from captivity to Jerusalem, the revelation, the prophets, and the miracles "closed" for 400 years. When Jesus came to earth, new revelation, new prophets, and miracles became public information. Then, within a few centuries, another divine silence fell upon the world. Yet silence was broken after a thousand years. And today, miracles are again occurring, though they may differ in kind and scope.

Today in place of a few men going around the world and performing many kinds of miracles, God has given all of us the privilege of seeing some miracles take place through our prayers (safety miracles, financial miracles, health miracles). Missionaries have testified that God has used them on occasion to cast out demons. J. Oswald Sanders writes, "If miraculous happenings sometimes occur in missionary work today, it is largely because in those areas conditions closely resemble those faced by the early church. In countries long enlightened by the gospel, miracles are not so necessary. This is a realm in which we cannot dictate to the sovereignty of God.[1]

observations

In order to have a balanced attitude toward miracles, we should keep several things in mind.

    1. *Miracles don't guarantee faith.* As a child I used to imag-

---

[1] J. Oswald Sanders, *The Holy Spirit and His Gifts* (Grand Rapids: Zondervan, 1970), p. 120.

ine the excitement of walking with Jesus when he was on earth. I saw the crowds gather around a blind man as Jesus touched the man's eyes. I saw the astonished look of the mourners as Lazarus walked from his tomb. And then I would wonder why God didn't do the same thing today. People would believe him immediately if miracles took place today as in the first century.

But the history of miracles denies that assumption. Moses performed ten great miracles before Pharaoh, but Pharaoh didn't believe. Jesus performed hundreds of miracles, but men crucified him for blasphemy. Peter and John healed a lame man, and the city council questioned, "What shall we do with these men? For the fact that a noteworthy miracle has taken place through them is apparent to all who live in Jerusalem, and we cannot deny it" (Acts 4:16). But did they believe in Jesus? Did they repent of their sins? No. They concluded, "But in order that it may not spread any further among the people, let us warn them to speak no more to any man in this name" (Acts 4:17).

Further, in Jesus' account of the rich man and Lazarus, the rich man pleads with Abraham to send a man back from the dead and warn his brothers not to come to the place of torment. Abraham replies, "If they do not listen to Moses and the Prophets [the way the Jews divided the Old Testament], neither will they be persuaded if someone rises from the dead" (Luke 16:31).

The proof of that statement is demonstrated by the reaction of the Jewish leaders after they were told of Jesus' resurrection. "And when they [the chief priests] had assembled with the elders and counseled together, they gave a large sum of money to the soldiers, and said, 'You are to say, "His disciples came by night and stole Him away while we were asleep." ' And they took the money and did as they had been instructed; and this story was widely spread among the Jews, and is to this day" (Matthew 28:12, 13, 15).

2. *Miracles won't increase faith.* A miracle is a supernatural power that appeals to the eyes more than to the will. It is an act to be seen. And many who see one great act want to see another and another without committing themselves to God. The scribes and Pharisees wanted to see a sign from Jesus but he replied, "An evil and adulterous generation craves for a sign" (Matthew 12:39).

Well-meaning Christians deceive themselves into thinking that if only they saw more miracles they would be more committed to Christ. They feel their faith would be increased. An individual who depends on the sign gifts (miracles, tongues, healings, and interpretation) for greater faith is one who is walking by sight rather than faith. Jesus told Thomas, "Blessed are they who did not see, and yet believed" (John 20:29).

3. *All miracles aren't of God.* When Moses stood before Pharaoh and Aaron cast the rod to the floor, it became a serpent. Not to be outdone, the magicians of Pharaoh's court threw their rods to the floor, and their rods also became serpents.

Jesus predicted that during the "tribulation" false prophets and a false messiah would appear who would be able to perform miracles. The signs they perform would be so convincing that, if possible, even the elect would be misled (Matthew 24:24).

The Apostle John predicted that in this same period two beast-like men will deceive mankind. One will be a political leader and the other a religious leader. John reveals that the religious leader "performs great signs, so that he even makes fire come down out of heaven to the earth in the presence of men. And he deceives those who dwell on the earth *because of the signs* which it was given him to perform" (Revelation 13:13, 14).

We can expect God to perform miracles to encourage and strengthen the person who is already committed to Jesus Christ and this may authenticate God's existence to some, but we should not depend upon miracles to do this. God exists whether or not spectacular events take place.

What about your life? Haven't you experienced times of drought? Haven't you had your fill of frustration? I'm sure you have. But even during those days, the promise of God stands firm: "Blessed is the man who trusts in the Lord and whose trust is the Lord. For he will be like a tree planted by the water, that extends its roots by a stream, and will not fear when the heat comes; but its leaves will be green, and *it will not be anxious in a year of drought* nor cease to yield fruit" (Jeremiah 17:7, 8).

The greatest miracle you can experience is the miracle of birth—the new birth (John 3:3). When that miracle takes place in your life you'll be prepared to tell another, "Hey, buddy, God's alive!"

THE GIFTS OF TONGUES AND INTERPRETATION

Few claims have had as much effect on the Christian world today as the claim that one possesses the biblical gift of speaking in tongues. This assumption has exhilarated many, divided others, and brought suspicion upon large segments of believers in various denominations.

Some Christians claim that a "tongues experience" is the basic factor for a believer's spiritual life. It's the sign of being baptized by the Holy Spirit. Dennis and Rita Bennett write, "What if I don't speak in tongues? Can I receive the Holy Spirit without speaking in tongues? It comes with the package! Speaking in tongues is not the baptism of the Holy Spirit, but it is what happens when and as you are baptized in the Spirit, and it becomes an important resource to help you continue, as Paul says, to 'be being (or keep on being) filled with the Holy Spirit' (Ephesians 5:18)."[2]

Other groups strongly react to this view and strictly forbid anyone to speak in tongues. They wouldn't say that God can't give this gift today, but they're convinced that he *hasn't* done so. Therefore, every experience of tongues-speaking is either a result of demon influence or psychological suggestion.[3] The result of these opposing views has been confusion, division, and dogmatism. When I've spoken to friends about the importance of spiritual gifts, a common reaction is either suspicion of my theology or a question about where I stand on the tongues issue.

As in the days of the early church, tongues have been counterfeited and abused by many. Yet some who practice tongues-speaking seem to understand and use tongues in a way comparable to the teaching of Scripture: the gift of tongues involves either a human language or an ecstatic utterance, unknown to the speaker (Acts 2:1–11), and it's a gift *not* given to all believers (1 Corinthians 12:10, 30).

I want to share several observations from the testimonies of

2 Dennis and Rita Bennett, *The Holy Spirit and You* (Plainfield, N.J.: Logos, 1971), p. 64.
3 For example: Robert G. Gromacki, *The Modern Tongues Movement* (Philadelphia: Presbyterian & Reformed Publishing Co., 1967).

some who have spoken in tongues, and from Paul's central passage on tongues (1 Corinthians 12–14). Then I will present several biblical principles on the use of tongues in public.

1. If you believe tongues-speaking is the norm, you should be aware that *the gift of tongues is reported in Acts only three times,* each a special occasion.

The Jews at Pentecost (Acts 2:3, 4). "And there appeared to them tongues as of fire distributing themselves, and they rested on each one of them. And they were all filled with the Holy Spirit and began to speak with other tongues, as the Spirit was giving them utterance."

The Gentiles (Acts 10:46). "For they were hearing them speaking with tongues and exalting God."

The disciples of John the Baptist (Acts 19:6). "And when Paul had laid his hands upon them, the Holy Spirit came upon them, and they began speaking with tongues and prophesying."

Each of these three times tongues occurred as a known language. And on each occasion God's message was introduced to a new group of people. In other words, tongues-speaking seemed to be the exception, not the rule.

2. It was *a gift of which Paul spoke only once,* and that was because of its abuse (1 Corinthians 12–14). Paul's message was not "Be saved, be baptized with the Holy Spirit, and speak in tongues." He preached Christ crucified, buried, and resurrected. When he spoke to Christians he didn't tell them to speak in tongues. Nor did he rebuke any man for not speaking in tongues. However, he did reprimand the misuse and overexaggeration of the gift. "However, in the church I desire to speak five words with my mind, that I may instruct others also, rather than ten thousand words in a tongue" (1 Corinthians 14:19).

3. A third observation concerns the authority by which some people justify their experience of tongues. *Some people's authority seems to be experience rather than doctrine.* Many of those who make use of this gift have a surface knowledge of the Scriptures. Their emphasis isn't on the whole counsel of God, but rather on the gift. They speak little about theology or doctrine. They emphasize their experiences.

Several charismatic books give procedures on how to speak

in tongues. The reader is told to start with a very simple sound and then to repeat it several times. As he repeats it, he should increase the tempo.[4]

4. *Those who speak in tongues claim that it helps their faith.* It may make them feel better, it may even make them feel closer to God, but does it increase faith? The faith of some may be increased by speaking in tongues. But it may require greater faith to believe God's truth when nothing visibly spectacular happens. Faith is described in Hebrews 11:1. "Now faith means putting our full confidence in the things we hope for; it means *being certain of things we cannot see*" (Phillips).

5. *Those who demand that all use tongues are in error* (1 Corinthians 12:10). The Scriptures say that different gifts are given to various believers. "And to another the effecting of miracles, and to another prophecy, and to another the distinguishing of spirits, to another various kinds of tongues, and to another the interpretation of tongues."

6. *Tongues-speaking did not always accompany Spirit-filling or (as some identify it) Spirit-baptism.* Although arguments from silence aren't the most convincing, notice the times when tongues-speaking is conspicuously absent. Peter was filled with the Holy Spirit but did not speak in tongues as he appeared before the Sanhedrin (Acts 4:8). The believers who met together for prayer were filled with the Holy Spirit. But rather than speaking in tongues, they spoke the Word of God with boldness (Acts 4:31). No indication is given that the seven deacons spoke in tongues, yet they were all filled with the Holy Spirit (Acts 6:5). Although Stephen (one of the seven) apparently never spoke with tongues, he "was performing great wonders and signs among the people" (Acts 6:8). Another time when the Bible refers to Stephen being filled with the Holy Spirit, his message was this: "Behold, I see the heavens opened up and the Son of Man standing at the right hand of God" (Acts 7:55, 56). If every Spirit-filled man could speak in tongues, Stephen could have used tongues as a sign to unbelievers. Either he didn't have the gift or he chose not to use it at this opportune time. One other account of Spirit-filling with-

4 Bennett, *op. cit.,* pp. 71–73.

out the accompanying sign of tongues is found in Acts 13:52. Here it states that the disciples at Antioch "were continually filled with joy and with the Holy Spirit."

7. *Tongues is one of the gifts readily counterfeited and thus subject to lack of control.* The use of tongues in 1 Corinthians 12 and 14 was apparently not counterfeit, but it was getting out of control. This is why Paul urged, "But let all things be done properly and in an orderly manner." Further, even those who speak in tongues recognize how easily the gift can be counterfeited. "All the gifts have their Satanic counterfeit, and there are certainly strange utterances and sounds made by those who worship other gods, or are involved in other religions or cults, that are counterfeits of speaking in tongues. In a large public meeting, where it is difficult to control the situation, it might be possible for such a person to manifest a counterfeit."[5]

Four possible sources of speaking in tongues are the divine, Satanic, psychological, or artificial. Today, I believe we are witnessing the practice of speaking in tongues as it originates from all four of these sources.

8. An eighth observation focuses on *the commands of Scripture.* Though there are many imperatives in Scripture, there is no command to speak in tongues. In contrast to this silence there are two major exhortations for every believer.

Paul wrote to the Ephesian believers, "I, therefore, the prisoner of the Lord, entreat you to walk in a manner worthy of the calling with which you have been called . . . being diligent to preserve the unity of the Spirit in the bond of peace . . ." (Ephesians 4:1, 3).

Some well-meaning but overzealous Christians sacrifice unity in order to propagate their experience. Paul informs us that a proper walk of the Christian is only achieved as he maintains unity.

However, as in a marriage relationship, so the preservation of unity in the Body of Christ means that both those who use tongues and those who do not are responsible to keep the unity of the Spirit.

5 *Ibid.,* p. 97.

Dr. Clark Pinnock's insightful article in *Christianity Today* describes the problem precisely. "It is commonly charged that the new Pentecostalism breeds division in the church . . . Undoubtedly some of the blame may be attributed to the movement for failing to show that all its emphases were unequivocally biblical. But the greater problem lies with the non-Pentecostal evangelicals themselves. We have not taken the movement seriously as a work of the Spirit of God. At best we have tolerated new Pentecostals in our churches, at worst driven them out. We have not exercised mature Christian leadership in this matter. It is high time that evangelical leaders begin to think about how to integrate the charismatic movement into the life of the Church and stop treating its members as spiritual lepers."[6]

A second important command was given to the disciples that last night of Jesus' earthly ministry. "A new commandment I give to you, that you love one another" (John 13:34). The use of tongues, like the use of any other gift, must be placed in subjection to one's love for others. If your use of tongues offends a body of believers, refrain from using your liberty to speak within that group (Romans 14:13–20). Likewise, if a brother desires to use his gift and an interpreter exists, you who don't have the gift should demonstrate your love by allowing him to exercise his gift and by responding to it in love. Forbidding one to speak in tongues may be just as unloving as demanding one's right to speak in tongues. Paul's exhortation is appropriate for proper balance: "Pursue love" (1 Corinthians 14:1).

9. A ninth observation from the Scriptures is the all-important emphasis placed on Christians *being Christlike*. True spirituality has no inherent relationship to the exercise of any of the spiritual gifts. The Holy Spirit produces his fruit in the believer's life. In so doing, he brings us into conformity with the image of Christ.

If you possess this gift I would encourage you to consider the following biblical teachings:

1. Recognize that an emphasis on the gift of tongues as being

6 Clark Pinnock, "The New Pentecostalism: Reflections by a Well-wisher, *Christianity Today* (September 14, 1973), p. 10.

central to the issue of *personal spirituality* is not biblical (1 Corinthians 12:28). In fact, the Holy Spirit will not draw attention to himself in the life of the believer but will focus the Christian's attention on Jesus Christ. "He will not speak of himself . . ." (John 16:13). Paul wrote, "Greater is one who prophesies than one who speaks in tongues" (1 Corinthians 14:5).

2. Recognize also that the gift of tongues, when not interpreted, doesn't build up the *Body of Christ*. It's a gift that *edifies the speaker rather than the audience* (1 Corinthians 14:4, 5). Therefore, a meeting centered on the use of "ecstatic utterances" for the benefit of the Christian community is inconsistent with the teaching of Scripture.

3. Tongues are said to be *a sign to the unbeliever*. It would be more profitable if tongues were used for evangelistic purposes than for edification purposes.[7]

4. Paul also teaches that if tongues are used in public, *an interpreter* must be present. If there is no interpreter, you are to remain silent (1 Corinthians 14:28). If there is an interpreter, only one person should speak at a time and each in turn (1 Corinthians 14:27). In fact, the apostle allowed only two or (at the most) three persons to use tongues at a meeting. This isn't a harsh rule. It was established so the rest of the Body of Christ could take part in the meeting.

The same rule is laid down for those who have the gift of prophecy. "And let two or three prophets speak, and let the others pass judgment" (1 Corinthians 14:29). Overuse of prophecy or ecstatic utterances in a meeting is not biblical. Paul's emphasis is on the entire local body of believers using their gifts to build up that body. "What is the outcome then, brethren? When you assemble, each one has a psalm, has a teaching, has a revelation, has a tongue, has an interpretation. Let all things be done for edification" (1 Corinthians 14:26).

5. Some tongues-speakers border on the point of preaching *"another gospel."* Recently I was invited to hear a man give his testimony. I'd been told he'd had a wonderful conversion experi-

7 Bennett, *op. cit.*, p. 86.

ence. His testimony lasted about one half hour and centered around his experience of "baptism in the Spirit." He said nothing about the new birth, the blood of Christ, or the need to receive Jesus Christ as personal Savior. He preached another gospel.

A friend of mine was sharing the conversion experiences of several persons he knew. Again the name of Christ wasn't even used. "She received the baptism in her own home. He got the baptism at our church." This was my friend's way of relating the new birth. Paul's message wasn't, "Be baptized by the Spirit," but "Believe on the Lord Jesus and you shall be saved" (Acts 16:30, 31).

6. Finally, *if you don't have the gift of tongues,* don't worry about it. Don't think of yourself as a second-class citizen. Thank God for the gifts you have. Paul writes, "All do not speak with tongues, do they? All do not interpret, do they? But earnestly desire the *greater gifts:* (1 Corinthians 12:30–31).

Hal Lindsey summarizes the polarization over the gift of tongues: "The charismatic movement has placed an unbalanced emphasis on the importance of tongues. They have drawn unscriptural conclusions about a genuine and bona fide spiritual gift. The more the Christian world has criticized their movement, the greater the claims they have made for tongues. The more they have sought to validate their emphasis with biblically unsupportable claims, the more conservative biblical scholars and Christians have resisted them.

"With a polarization like this, who do you think is the winner? You guessed it! Satan. He goads both sides on in their causes and then stands back and laughs while they battle each other instead of him."[8]

God is not glorified when we battle one another. Spiritual gifts aren't to be used as weapons, but are tools for God's glory. I plead for tolerance. "I beg you . . . to live and act in a way worthy of those who have been chosen for such wonderful blessings as these. Be humble and gentle. Be patient with each other; making allowance for each other's faults because of your love. Try

8 Lindsey, *op. cit.,* pp. 147, 148.

always to be led along together by the Holy Spirit, and so be at peace with one another" (Ephesians 4:1–3, TLB).

what are your gifts?

In his booklet *How to Be Filled with the Spirit,* [1] Dr. Bill Bright tells the story of a famous oil field known as Yates Pool. "During the depression this field was a sheep ranch owned by a man named Yates. Mr. Yates wasn't able to make enough on his ranching operation to pay the principal and interest on the mortgage, so he was in danger of losing his ranch. With little money for clothes or food, his family (like many others) had to live on government subsidy.

"Day after day, as he grazed his sheep over those rolling West Texas hills, he was no doubt greatly troubled about how he would pay his bills. Then a seismographic crew from an oil company came into the area and told him that there might be oil on his land. They asked permission to drill a wildcat well and he signed a lease contract.

"At 1,115 feet they struck a huge oil reserve. The first well came in at 80,000 barrels a day. Many subsequent wells were more than twice as large. In fact, 30 years after the discovery, a government test of one of the wells showed that it still had the potential flow of 125,000 barrels of oil a day. And Mr. Yates owned it all. The day he purchased the land he had received the

1 Available from Campus Crusade for Christ, Arrowhead Springs, San Bernardino, Calif.

oil and mineral rights. Yet, he'd been living on relief. A multimillionaire living in poverty! The problem? He didn't know the oil was there, even though he owned it."

Many Christians have a similar problem. They live in spiritual poverty, unaware of the potential that God has given them. They're unaware of the gifts of the Holy Spirit that they have.

How can you know what gifts God has given you? Can you follow certain procedures to discover which ones you have? Yes, it's possible and, in fact, expected that you will discern them. God doesn't play hide and seek with his children. He wants you to see yourself as he sees you.

FAITH

The search begins with faith. You must believe that you are gifted.

Too often Christians view spiritual gifts as wishful thinking. They see them as special rewards for the spiritual elite. They feign humility and conclude that God hasn't seen fit to so endow them. Yet they attempt to serve him the best they can, in spite of their inabilities.

God doesn't ask man to do what he hasn't equipped him to do. Listen to what Jesus says to his disciples. "You didn't choose me! I chose you! I appointed you to go and produce lovely fruit always, so that no matter what you ask for from the Father, using my name, he will give it to you" (John 15:16, TLB). But how can man produce the fruit of God? Isn't that an impossible task? Yes, it is, except for one condition. Jesus explains that condition like this. "Take care to live in me, and let me live in you. For a branch can't produce fruit when severed from the vine. Nor can you be fruitful apart from me" (v. 4). The condition is to abide in the source of spiritual power. If the believer abides in Christ, he will produce spiritual fruit.

Likewise, we are to serve God with the gifts he has provided for us. Paul writes, "But *to each one* is given the manifestation of the Spirit for the common good" (1 Corinthians 12:7). Peter confirms this by writing, "As *each one* has received a special gift, employ it in serving one another" (1 Peter 4:10).

Either it's true that you are gifted or the Bible is false in its claim. You must decide. And if you have difficulty in believing it because you lack experience, then believe it because the Bible teaches it as truth. Accept it by faith. *You are gifted.* Thank God for the gifts he has given you and continue your search. You are now prepared to take the second step in your quest.

PRAYER

The second step centers around prayer. The Lord has already given us a means to discover the unknown. "You do not have because you do not ask" (James 4:2). Pray for understanding.

"But I have asked God to show me my gift. I want to know what it is." Perhaps you have asked God this. Perhaps you have a desire to know. But your gifts may still be hidden because of wrong motives. James continues his statement by writing, "You ask and do not receive, because you ask with wrong motives, so that you may spend it on your pleasures" (James 4:3).

You may have a friend who is obviously gifted. He receives the acclaim of others. He is popular. He is successful. And in your heart you'd give anything to have his gifts and popularity. And so you ask God to show you quickly what he has given you, so that you too might find acceptance among the group. This is hardly an acceptable motive. It's about like the motive of Simon, the converted sorcerer. "Now when Simon saw that the Spirit was bestowed through the laying on of the apostles' hands, he offered them money, saying, 'Give this authority to me as well, so that everyone on whom I lay my hands may receive the Holy Spirit.' But Peter said to him, 'May your silver perish with you, because you thought you could obtain the gift of God with money! You have no part or portion in this matter, for your heart is not right before God. Therefore, repent of this wickedness of yours, and pray the Lord that if possible, the intention of your heart may be forgiven you. For I see that you are in the gall of bitterness and in the bondage of iniquity.' But Simon answered and said, 'Pray to the Lord for me yourselves, so that nothing of what you have said may come upon me' " (Acts 8:18, 24).

Why do you want to know your gifts? It may not be to compete with your friends, but for another wrong motive. Some Christians approach God in prayer like this: "Lord, I'm really curious about my gifts. I never realized I was gifted. But now I believe I am. So I'd appreciate your showing me what my gifts are. I'm really curious." If this is your attitude, don't be surprised that you never discover your gifts.

God doesn't want us to pray for understanding in order to satisfy our curiosity. He wants us to ask with commitment. Our attitude must be, "Lord, show me my gifts so I can begin to develop and use them." That's commitment. Tell the Lord you'll use your gifts as he reveals them to you. Be prepared for him to open your eyes to some exciting potential. You'll soon find opportunities for service.

AWARENESS

Besides faith and prayer, there is a third step in understanding gifts: awareness. Be aware of what gifts are available to you.

The purpose of this book is to make you aware of the available gifts. You may already have identified with several of the gifts that have been discussed. But to help you review, I have tried to categorize the eighteen or more gifts in the Scriptures according to their emphasis. Some relate to helping others. Some relate closely to the use of Scripture. Some emphasize directing others. And some call attention to themselves in ways that are spectacular.

ministry of helping

1. *Serving*—the ability to give assistance or aid in any way that brings strength or encouragement to others.
2. *Giving*—the ability to make and distribute money to further the cause of God.
3. *Showing Mercy*—the ability to work joyfully with those whom the majority ignores.
4. *Craftsmanship*—the ability to work with one's hands for the benefit of others.

5. *Healings*—the ability to heal a person spiritually, emotionally, or physically.

ministry of directing others

1. *Leadership* (Administration)—the ability to lead others and manage the affairs of the church.
2. *Faith*—the ability to trust God beyond the probable and raise the vision of others.

ministry of the word

These gifts have a direct relation with the Scriptures.

1. *Apostleship*—the ability to begin a new work for the Lord through the ministry of the Word.
2. *Prophecy*—the ability to proclaim or preach the Word of God.
3. *Evangelism*—the ability to present Christ in such a way that men usually respond by faith.
4. *Pastor-Teacher*—the ability to care for a man's spiritual needs through teaching the Word of God. The ability to nurture others in truth.
5. *Teaching*—the ability to analyze and interpret God's truth and communicate it clearly and systematically.
6. *Exhortation*—the ability to motivate people to action, normally using the authority of God's Word.
7. *Wisdom*—the ability to apply God's truth to life.
8. *Knowledge*—the ability to know truth by the impression of the Holy Spirit.
9. *Discernment of spirits*—the ability to discern the spirits of truth and error.
10. *Music*—the ability to express one's relationship to God through music.

ministry of the spectacular

(I wasn't sure in which category to place the last three gifts. So, since they often call attention to themselves, I use the term *spectacular*.)

1. *Miracles*—the ability to perform acts contrary to natural laws, with power beyond human capacity.
2. *Tongues*—the ability to speak in a language unlearned by the speaker.
3. *Interpretation*—the ability to interpret the meaning of a tongue, though the interpreter hasn't learned the language.

RESPONSIBILITY

In what type of service are you presently involved? You may be a Sunday school teacher, youth sponsor, choir member, visitation chairman, or board member. Maybe you're using your gifts in a home Bible study, transportation, maintenance, or committee work. What is important is that you're involved in something. Why? Because as you serve the Lord, he'll show you what you can and cannot do. And it's possible that he will reveal new gifts to you.

Do you recall the life of Philip? He was a product of the early Jerusalem church which practiced a type of communal living. None of the believers in that congregation possessed personal property. There was equality of material goods. Luke describes it like this: "For there was not a needy person among them, for all who were owners of lands or houses would sell them and bring the proceeds of the sales, and lay them at the apostles' feet, and they would be distributed to each, as any had need" (Acts 4:34, 35).

This plan worked well for a period, but soon a problem arose. The Hellenistic Jews complained that the native Jews were discriminating against their widows. The Hellenistic Jewish widows were being deprived of "their portion."

Recognizing the problem, the apostles challenged the congregation to elect seven men to administrate the daily distribution. Their qualifications were to be their character and gifts: their good reputation and Spirit-filled life (Acts 6:3). Their spiritual gifts probably included the gift of wisdom ("full . . . of wisdom"), the gift of administration ("put in charge"), and the gift of helps ("this task" of distributing food).

Philip was one of the "Jerusalem seven," and thus was demonstrating the gifts of wisdom, administration, and helps. Then a great persecution spread throughout Jerusalem. The ringleader of the persecution was Saul of Tarsus. He entered house after house and dragged men and women off to jail. Christians began to flee for their lives. And as they fled through Judea and Samaria they preached Christ.

Philip was no exception. He left Jerusalem and went down to Samaria. Like the other believers he preached Christ. And while he was preaching, it became apparent that he had three other gifts. The great response to his preaching showed that he had the gifts of prophecy and evangelism. "But when they believed Philip *preaching* the good news about the kingdom of God and the name of Jesus Christ, they were being baptized, men and women alike" (Acts 8:12). In fact, in Acts 21:8 he is called Philip the *evangelist.* And then a sixth gift was discovered as he continued his ministry, the gift of miracles. "And the multitudes with one accord where giving attention to what was said by Philip, as they heard and saw the signs which he was performing. . . . And even Simon himself believed; . . . as he observed signs and great *miracles* taking place, he was constantly amazed" (Acts 8:6, 13). As Philip accepted responsibility, God revealed more gifts to him.

And as you accept new responsibilities, God will reveal other gifts to you that were previously hidden. However, two problems keep many Christians from discovering their gifts.

lack of variety

The first problem is lack of variety in experience. Perhaps for the past five years or more you've been teaching Sunday school. You may have been very successful. You may be satisfied with your gift of teaching. But it's possible that other gifts will be uncovered if you take on a different responsibility for a while. Consider accepting a new challenge.

George and Jean were youth sponsors for several years. They

enjoyed teen-agers and vice versa. Then one day Jean's pastor asked her to head the Vacation Bible School program, a challenge she accepted with apprehension. But during the next few years she demonstrated her gift of leadership so successfully that other churches turned to her for advice. A new challenge uncovered a new gift.

refusal to relocate

A second problem that limits our discovery of gifts is refusal to change responsibility when it's evident we're not equipped for some task. You may be facing insurmountable problems in your present responsibility. You don't know where to turn. You don't feel equipped to continue. And you feel frustrated because, if you quit, people may question your spirituality or perseverance. So you continue to teach, lead, visit, and become more frustrated.

Don't be afraid to "relocate." Quitting isn't the answer. To leave your responsibility and sit on the bench will neither help you discover your gifts nor help the Lord's work. But relocating might surprise you.

If you seem to be a failure at teaching junior high students, try another age group or another responsibility altogether. If you feel inadequate in your position of leadership, think about giving the responsibility to someone who can lead and then offer to help.

No one has to feel like a failure. It's no disgrace to fail in a ministry to which God has never called you. But it's a disgrace to live in failure and refuse to consider another area of service.

If my church board ever came to me and asked me to be in charge of maintenance and mechanical work, I'd become a colossal failure. It isn't that I don't want to get my hands dirty. The problem I would face is knowing where to start and how to do what needed to be done. My mechanical ability is limited, and I'd be in a state of continuous frustration. On the other hand, it would be wrong for me to conclude that because I'm a failure in mechanics I therefore can do nothing in the church. The answer to my problem would be to relocate. I'd be wise to turn the mechanical responsibility over to someone else and accept a responsibility I can both enjoy and do more effectively.

COMMON SENSE

A fifth approach to the problem of discovering your gifts is common sense. Sometimes we tend to think that common sense is unspiritual. We want God to reveal his gifts to us in some extraordinary way. Common sense is so unspectacular. But common sense comes from God, and he expects us to use it in discovering our gifts. Here are four areas in which you can use common sense.

1. Consider your *desires*. What do you enjoy doing? To what are you drawn? What seems to come naturally to you? Some Christians fail to recognize their gifts because they use them without effort.

The craftsman, for instance, may think that working with his hands or drawing pictures is so easy that anyone can do it. But this isn't true. The person with the gift of helps may think, "Doesn't every woman enjoy cooking?" "Doesn't everyone have the same desire to help?" "Doesn't every man enjoy ushering?" Or, the individual with the gift of leadership wonders, "Why aren't there more leaders? Anyone can lead if he only tries."

2. Consider the *needs of others*. What need do you see that you want to do something about? Perhaps you believe that one of the great needs today is to minister to the lonely, sick, mentally retarded, or socially deprived. You may have often asked yourself, "What can I do to help them?" It's quite possible that you have the gift of showing mercy.

Among other gifts, I believe my wife Linda possesses the gift of mercy. She constantly wonders what she can do to help people in need. When she sees a lonely person she goes out of her way to make him feel wanted. She has worked with the socially deprived. Her heart is warm toward the physically, mentally, socially, or emotionally handicapped.

You may not react that way around handicapped people. But you may enter a business, a school, or a church, and the first thing you notice is the lack of organization, poor policy, or inefficient methods in handling problems. You can't stand chaos. You want to make changes. It's quite possible that you possess the gift of leadership or administration.

Or perhaps you have a burning desire to see people come to

Christ. When you think of your friends you realize they're without him. You do a lot of personal evangelism. You share your faith because the reality of the lost is so vivid to you. You love to tell others about Christ, and you've introduced many to him. That is strong evidence for the gift of evangelism.

3. Consider your *experience.* What past ministries have you enjoyed? In what areas of service have you already had some success?

For instance, you may have been a successful camp counselor. Some children came to Christ, while others were helped by your encouragement and love. The gift of exhortation is closely linked with counseling, since it includes giving comfort, encouraging, and rebuking. Your gift may be undeveloped at present, but the potential exists.

Perhaps your experiences have centered around working on cars, taking gadgets apart and putting them back together, carpentry work, designing, or decorating. Interest and skill in these areas may mean that you have the gift of craftsmanship.

"But doesn't this imply that one must be an adult before he can discover his gifts? A child certainly wouldn't have these experiences." I disagree. When I think of craftsmanship I recall a teen-ager in Pennsylvania. Ever since he was small, he's been interested in mechanical equipment. His father and grandfather were proficient in working with their hands, so this boy was continuously exposed to machines, screwdrivers, soldering irons, and transformers. At the age of thirteen, he is already a good mechanic. He enjoys this type of work and seems to have the gift of craftsmanship.

Parents have opportunity to observe the desires and tendencies of their children. By encouraging them to develop their "natural skills" they can help them discover God's gifts.

4. Another help in discovering your gifts is the *confirmation of others.* What do others say about you? In what area do people look up to you? What have you done in the past for which you were genuinely complimented? Are you known as a serious student? You may have the gift of teaching. Are you known as one who says the right thing at the right time? You may have the gift of wisdom. Do people with serious problems tend to come to you? You probably have the gift of helps or serving.

In contrast, if you're always attempting to lead others, but no one follows your leadership, reconsider your gift. If you sing and never receive positive feedback, look elsewhere for your gift. If you're teaching and students stay away in droves, think about doing something else.

God wants you to discover your gifts. You will, if you begin with faith, pray, recognize what gifts are available, accept responsibility, and use your common sense.

putting your gifts to use

One of the most exciting gifts I received as a child was a new bicycle. I was playing several blocks away from my house when suddenly a friend came running down the street shouting, "Ricky! Ricky! Guess what! I saw a truck pull up to your house and it had two new bikes in the back. And your dad helped the man unload them."

I yelled to my sister who was playing nearby and we ran home like jack rabbits. When we arrived, our mouths dropped open. Right before us stood two shiny new bikes. And they were ours.

At that point, the only obstacle facing me was learning to ride. I'd been on a bike only a few times, but within days, I was riding my new bike as if I'd been born on it.

This may be where you are right now. You've discovered what may be your gifts. You may be excited about your finding. And now you must learn how to use them effectively. Here are three fundamental principles to help you develop your discoveries.

TAKE ADVANTAGE OF OPPORTUNITIES

We could all be more effective teachers, singers, leaders, visitors, counselors, maintenance workers, and witnesses if we would take advantage of learning and training opportunities available.

training classes

Suppose you have the gift of leadership, but it is not at all developed. You want to learn how to lead and administrate. Perhaps your church holds leadership classes, or an evening school in your community offers administration courses. Sign up and see what happens.

If you have the gift of teaching or at least want to investigate the possibility, let this be known. Attend every teachers' meeting in your church, if they are available. Publishing houses often go into a community and offer one-day or weekend seminars. A leader or teacher who fails to attend training sessions hurts both himself and his ministry. There is always room for improvement.

If your gift is music, you will improve tremendously if you try to take private lessons and practice every day. If not that, you can still practice on your own or play or sing with groups. Choir rehearsals in many churches are more than practice for Sunday morning. They are times of training and improving voice quality. We should give God our best, rather than what is left over of our time and gifts. So look for some training program in your church or community and take advantage of it.

reading

Do you realize that only 23 percent of the Christian public ever reads a book? Recently I talked with a friend from a Christian publishing company and asked him who reads their books. He replied that the progressive contemporary evangelical and the progressive contemporary liberal read most of the Christian literature. The hardened liberal (who denies everything and refuses to have anyone change his mind) along with the dogmatic fundamentalist (who has solved all the world's problems) do other things with their time. And then he added that about 80 percent of the readers are women. That's quite a commentary on the reading habits of the religious public. No wonder many Christians don't grow in their spiritual lives. If they don't supplement their

Sunday diet with good reading material, their Christian vision remains embryonic.

Every gift that is found in the Scriptures can be developed through reading. You may say, "But I'm just a mechanic." Well, you can read magazines like *Popular Mechanics* to improve your gift. Read books on how to be a more effective teacher. Biographies of people like Helen Keller may challenge you to develop your gift of showing mercy. The biography of LeTourneau, Kresge, J. C. Penney, or John Wanamaker may stimulate you to use your gift of giving. Biographies of William Carey and other missionaries may ripen your gift of apostleship. A biography of George Müller will encourage your gift of faith.

You may not be able to attend a lot of training sessions or go back to school, but you can read. And if reading is agony because you're so slow, there are reading courses to help increase both speed and comprehension. It all depends on how serious you are with God. How committed are you to use your gifts?

conferences

Conferences offer tremendous opportunity to develop gifts. A gifted teacher should attend Sunday school and V.B.S. workshops. When I was a Christian education director, I attended as many conferences as I could fit into my time and budget, because at these conferences I discovered new ideas and methods for teaching. You may want to improve your witness for Christ, or perhaps you want to know if you have the gift of evangelism. Try the various Lay Institutes for Evangelism throughout the U.S. and Canada. If you want to improve your leadership with youth, attend Bill Gothard's "Youth Conflicts" seminar.

school

Today many adults develop their gifts by going back to school. I'm not referring primarily to attending college as a full-time student, though in some cases this may be necessary. I'm thinking of night school or summer school, both of which offer an incredible number of possibilities.

tapes

Another means of improving spiritual gifts is the use of tapes. With the cassette boom you can get information on just about anything. There are tapes to help you improve your musical ability, leadership, evangelistic ability, etc. Some tapes merely present factual material while others provide "how to" information. You can listen to tapes as you would listen to a transistor radio, while walking to school, while preparing meals, while you sun-bathe, or drive to the mountains. You may not have time to read a book, but you can probably find time to listen to a tape.

These are some of the resources available to you for developing your gifts. Some are more expensive than others. Some are more time-consuming than others. But don't excuse yourself from taking advantage of some resource.

Don't be satisfied with what you now know, or with past performance. Strive for excellence. Seek to improve. That's what growth and maturity mean.

EXERCISE YOUR GIFT

It's evident that we can develop *knowledge* by reading, listening, and visualizing, but *gifts* and *skills* can be developed only by use. Ability grows as you put your gift to work. It's like a muscle. Neglect it and it becomes weak and flabby. Use it and it will perform usefully.

RECOGNIZE VALUE

This principle is especially helpful when your motivation is low. If you feel depressed or discouraged, you'll have little desire to develop your gifts. But if you realize the advantages of developed gifts, your motivation may increase.

developed gifts provide personal identity

One of the major crises that most of us go through is the identity crisis. Who am I? Why am I here? Where am I going? This crisis has become a major problem in our depersonalized society.

God says that you are a gifted person with a divine mission on earth. You are necessary for the rest of the Body of Christ. And you will experience the truth of this as you discover your gifts and use them.

developed gifts remove unnecessary guilt

Each of us experiences guilt to some degree at various times. The Sunday school teacher who fails to prepare his lesson, the father who refuses to discipline his children, the young person who yells at his parents, the Christian who bypassed an opportunity to witness: these are everyday examples of guilt. Sometimes our guilt is justifiable and other times it's unnecessary.

In *Guilt and Grace,* Paul Tournier describes two kinds of guilt: "true guilt," which is the result of disobeying God, and "false guilt," which results from the judgments and suggestions of men. We may make people feel guilty because of the way they dress or look or waste time or relate to others. We set up standards and expect others to comply. When they fail to achieve our standards, they sense our judgment and feel guilty. False guilt may also come from failure to reach our own goals, even if they are unrealistic.

Men have entered the ministry because their parents or some friend convinced them this was God's will. Eventually they drop out, and may feel guilt about their failure the rest of their lives. Some Christians accept church responsibilities because others felt they should, and if they are unsuccessful, they develop guilt. However, once you understand that God has gifted you for certain tasks, and you fail where he hasn't gifted you, you have no reason for guilt. That is false guilt. It is unnecessary.

developed gifts help you become a pace-setter

Many Christians merely echo what they hear. Too few really think for themselves. They have little self-identity. In contrast, the Christian who develops and uses his gift becomes a pace-setter. He isn't competing with other Christians. He isn't wasting his time comparing his results with the results of others. Instead, he is accomplishing what God has equipped him to do. In striving for excellence with his gift, he sets the pace for others. When he speaks people listen. He may even become an authority in his field.

SUMMARY

As I conclude this chapter, I want to share a verse of Scripture that revolutionized my own attitude about God's working in my life. It has kept me from pushing ahead of God's time. It has removed the fear of "failing to make the grade." It has given me confidence that God has a place for me and will lead me in discovering it.

The passage is this: "A man's gift makes room for him, and brings him before great men" (Proverbs 18:16).

David's gift of music opened the door to Saul's palace. Philip's gifts of evangelism and miracles opened the door to Samaria. Paul's gifts of apostleship and teaching brought him to the Western world with the gospel. Elijah's gift of faith closed the heavens for three years, and brought him before King Ahab and the people of Israel. Bezalel's gift of craftsmanship built the tabernacle of God in the wilderness. Nathan's gift of prophecy brought him before David the king. Solomon's gift of wisdom brought great men and women of the world to his court. Peter's gift of exhortation caused 3,000 Jews to repent in a day.

God may not use your gift to bring you before great men. He may not use your gift in a way that the Christian world will sit back and admire. But be certain that he will open many doors for you to serve him.

"A man's gift makes room for him."

gifts and
the local church

Jesus has commissioned the church to "make disciples of all the nations" (Matthew 28:19). Some limit this statement to a ministry of evangelism. Others emphasize the educational ministry of the local church.

Another aspect of our commission includes helping individuals to discover, develop, and use their spiritual gifts, for it is through these that believers will be able to disciple others for Jesus. But most Christians are unaware of the biblical teachings about spiritual gifts and their relationship to the local church. Here are some of those principles.

GOD WANTS YOU TO KNOW
ABOUT YOUR SPIRITUAL GIFTS

"Now concerning spiritual gifts, brethren, I do not want you to be unaware" (1 Corinthians 12:1). But the tragedy of the average church is that its members don't know they are gifted. According to the Bible, every believer is gifted by the Holy Spirit (1 Peter 4:10). Yet, statistically speaking, do you think that 20 percent of these believers are using their gifts?

The Bible implies that there is to be only one kind of church member: an active member. A local church who holds on to an "inactive" membership list perpetuates the lie that it is proper to do nothing for the Lord. It hints that service is optional. It excuses some members from ever taking responsibility. It keeps believers from developing the gifts that God has given to them.

What happens when a church ignores the importance of spiritual gifts?

dissension may creep into the church

When members don't understand the biblical teaching of gifts, they may begin to compete with one another. Feelings are hurt because their work isn't acknowledged from the pulpit. A soloist may become embittered against the choir director because he or she hasn't been asked to sing as often as another soloist. Or perhaps a member strives for a board position or seeks to chair a committee. Yet it's obvious that his gift isn't administration. When he doesn't get elected, he holds a grudge against the entire membership or against the one who got "his" position.

program may become all-important

When the church's vision isn't on a man's spiritual gifts, it's usually on program. Instead of asking, "What needs do we have? What gifts do we have to meet our needs?" it asks, "What kind of exciting program can we offer to keep people coming?" The result is an entertainment binge, competing with other churches as well as with the professionalism of the world.

Good program isn't wrong. A local congregation should provide the best programs it can innovate. But program must be designed to meet need. Program must become the servant of the spiritual gifts of a church. In other words, *the gifts of the local body of Christ should determine the program of the church.*

Suppose God has blessed a congregation abundantly with the gift of music. One of the strong emphases of that church should be a program that develops and uses its members' musical gifts. So you see, local churches should be as distinct from one another as one person is different from another. Each should develop its own personality by the power of the Holy Spirit and make a unique contribution to its community.

Why are so many Christians unaware of their spiritual gifts? Perhaps one reason is that they fear fanaticism. Because the sign gifts (tongues, healing, miracles) are overemphasized by some groups, the fear arises that "something unusual or uncontrollable will happen if I dabble in spiritual gifts."

Another possible reason is that they lack information about all the other gifts available to Christians (showing mercy, faith, helps, administration, teaching, craftsmanship, etc.). In my research for this book I discovered very little written about these other gifts. (In fact, that's the reason for this book.)

Third, some Christians are unaware of their gifts because they lack commitment to Christ. A Christian may be gifted in music, but because he is lazy he refuses to practice. Or he may feel that if he just sings in church, voice lessons would be a waste of money. (In other words, anything is good enough for God.) Someone else may have the gift of administration. But he depends completely upon past experience. He never considers reading books on leadership or attending seminars that would help him develop his gift.

GIFTS HAVE TWO BASIC PURPOSES IN THE CHURCH

Gifts are to produce growth. "But to each one is given the manifestation of the spirit *for the common good* . . . So also you, since you are zealous of spiritual gifts, seek to abound *for the edification* of the church . . . Let all things be done *for edification*" (1 Corinthians 12:7; 14:12, 26). Gifts are not for one's private use. They are to be shared, not hoarded.

Another purpose of gifts is *to produce unity.* "That there should be no division in the body, but that the members should have the same care for one another" (1 Corinthians 12:25). The Holy Spirit has not given gifts to produce competition. His purpose was to produce contribution and thus a unity of spirit. This was the problem in Corinth. They had so exaggerated the effectiveness of the gift of tongues that those who didn't have it were looked upon as second-class citizens.

EACH MEMBER OF THE
BODY OF CHRIST IS NECESSARY

"For the body is not one member, but many. If the foot should say, 'Because I am not a hand, I am not a part of the body,' it is not for this reason any less a part of the body. And if the ear should say, 'Because I am not an eye, I am not a part of the body,' it is not for this reason any less a part of the body. If the whole body were an eye, where would the hearing be? If the whole were hearing, where would the sense of smell be? . . . And the eye cannot say to the hand, 'I have no need of you,' or again the head to the feet, 'I have no need of you' " (1 Corinthians 12:14–17, 29).

GIFTS DIFFER

"And God has appointed in the church, *first* apostles, *second* prophets, *third* teachers, *then* miracles, *then* gifts of healings, helps, administration, various kinds of tongues" (1 Corinthians 12:28).

Discrimination? Recall Paul's argument, "If the whole body were an eye, where would the hearing be? If the whole were hearing, where would the sense of smell be? But now *God has placed* the members, each one of them, in the body, *just as He desired*" (1 Corinthians 12:17, 18).

The feet might say, "The hands are higher than we are. It's not fair." Or the heart might say, "No one ever sees me unless they use some special instrument. I'm just not too important." True, some members of the body are more obvious. Some members are more vital to life than others. But each member is responsible to fulfill its own function.

MEMBERS DIFFER

"On the contrary, it is much truer that the members of the body which seem to be *weaker* are necessary; and those members of the body, which we deem *less honorable,* on those we bestow more abundant honor, and our *unseemly* members come to have more abundant seemliness, whereas our seemly members have no need of it. But God has so composed the body, giving more abundant honor to that member which lacked" (1 Corinthians 12:22–24).

Here, the Apostle Paul reveals the "pecking" order of the Christian world. "Oh, Charlie? Well, he doesn't do very much. He just comes around once in a while. I'd never miss him if he left." God's opinion is quite different. He says, "The members of the body which *seem* to be weaker [less important] are *necessary*." Our attitude is often so negative toward such persons that they seldom get opportunity or training to function properly.

In the body of Christ some members are obnoxious. Some are an embarrassment to others. Some aren't much to look at. James wrote like this about such matters: "My brethren do not hold your faith in our glorious Lord Jesus Christ with an attitude of personal favoritism. For if a man comes into your assembly with a gold ring and dressed in fine clothes, and there also comes in a poor man in dirty clothes, and you pay special attention to the one who is wearing the fine clothes, and say, 'You sit here in a good place,' and you say to the poor man, 'You stand over there, or sit down by my footstool,' have you not made distinctions among yourselves, and become judges with evil motives?" (James 2:1–4).

Or to use a more contemporary illustration, suppose one individual is stylishly dressed and well-groomed, but another is a hippie-type, long-haired and grubby. Are we partial? Do we judge with wrong motives?

there are those who are hidden or unnoticed

As certain parts of the body are concealed from public life, so parts of the body of Christ are concealed from public life. Paul encourages the unveiling of the hidden members of the spiritual body, the church: "Our unseemly [hidden] members come to have more abundant seemliness [exposure]" (1 Corinthians 12:23).

A magazine article[1] tells about Mrs. Beers, a widow who was stricken with multiple sclerosis many years ago. Her opportunities to work in the local church were limited and soon closed altogether. Her pastor suggested that she write letters to others who are passing through periods of great testing. She accepted the challenge and began to write. Mrs. Beers has averaged nearly 4,500 letters each year for the past twenty years. She receives an average of 2,000 replies each year. The results of changed lives have been astonishing.

Mrs. Beers was one of those members hidden away in a convalescent home, away from the public eye until someone from Scripture Press exposed her to the public. Hundred of other men and women perform similarly inconspicuous ministries. God sees and honors them, and at times brings them to the attention of someone who reveals their faithfulness to the public.

PROPER UNDERSTANDING OF SPIRITUAL GIFTS SHOULD ELIMINATE INFERIORITY FEELINGS

No matter how often you say that every member of the body of Christ is essential, there are those who cannot accept the fact. Some claim they're too old to be useful. Others claim they're not educated enough. Others say they're too young. But no matter what the claim, Paul argues: "If the foot should say, 'Because I am not a hand, I am not a part of the body,' it is not for this reason any the less a part of the body. And if the ear should say, 'Because I am not an eye, I am not a part of the body,' it is not for this reason any the less a part of the body" (1 Corinthians 12:15, 16).

This is self-deception. It's false humility. It's not only unbiblical, it's antibiblical. There is no need for anyone in the body of Christ to feel inferior.

Who has most influenced your life? Was it a young, well-

1 "90,000 Letters Later," *Power for Living* (January 23, 1972).

educated, dynamic person? Most likely it wasn't. And yet, most people expect to find spiritual gifts limited to such people.

PROPER UNDERSTANDING OF SPIRITUAL GIFTS SHOULD ELIMINATE EXAGGERATED SELF-ESTEEM

"And the eye cannot say to the hand, 'I have no need of you,' or again the head to the feet, 'I have no need of you' " (1 Corinthians 12:21). There are those in the church who consider themselves above the average church member. They are self-satisfied. They feel they've reached a level of maturity, ability, or knowledge far ahead of the rest. They sit back, relax, and coast along. They watch from the outside and pass down judgments of approval or disapproval on what is happening.

"For through the grace given to me I say to every man among you not to think more highly of himself than he ought to think; but to think so as to have sound judgment, as God has alloted to each a measure of faith" (Romans 12:3). When you use sound judgment you recognize your strengths and weaknesses. You accept and utilize your spiritual gifts. "For who regards you as superior? And what do you have that you did not receive? But if you did receive it, why do you boast as if you had not received it" (1 Corinthians 4:7). You may have greater intellectual capacity than the average church member. You may possess excellent insight. You may be more richly gifted. You may have a splendid personality. But where did you get this? From God. How, then, can you boast?

Someone might say, "I admit I can't brag about my gifts and my abilities. But I think I have some room to brag about what I've been able to accomplish for the Lord. I've done ten times as much as any other member in this congregation." If that is true you'll get your reward. God won't close his eyes to your good works. But until that great day, Jesus tells us to develop this attitude: "So you too, when you do all the things which are commanded you, say, 'We are unworthy slaves; we have done only that which we ought to have done' " (Luke 17:10).

SPIRITUAL GIFTS SHOULD BE USED TO HELP US CARE FOR ONE ANOTHER

"That there should be no division in the body, but that the members should have the same care for one another" (1 Corinthians 12:25). We care by sharing others' burdens. "Bear one another's burdens, and thus fulfill the law of Christ" (Galatians 6:2). This means that we have to become honest enough and humble enough to admit burdens and problems.

To share another's burdens includes praying for him. It might mean being available to counsel or to help in some material, physical, or spiritual way. I'm not advocating that you become an "ear" for hypochondriacs; some people have imaginary ailments who'd like nothing better than to spend hours telling you about them.

We can also care by confessing our sins to each other. If there is any area of life that Christians would like to bypass, it is confessing personal sin. And yet, this is a biblical exhortation. "Therefore, confess your sins to one another, and pray for one another, so that you may be healed. The effectual prayer of a righteous man can accomplish much" (James 5:16).

What does that mean? At the least it means that Christians should admit their weaknesses and failures as they live the Christian life. In the home, a father may have to apologize to his children because he blamed them for something they didn't do. He may ask his wife and children to pray that God will help him control his temper. A teen-ager may have to confess he wasn't where he told his parents he was last night. A student may have to confess to a teacher that he cheated on an exam and doesn't deserve the grade he received. A wife may have to confess to her husband that she has resented some of his habits all these years. Honest, open confession plus sincere prayer produces results.

A few years ago, a revival was sweeping across the Canadian provinces of Saskatchewan and Manitoba. People were confessing their faults to one another. Husbands and wives acknowledged their bitterness and self-centeredness. Men made restitution to employers whom they had cheated. One article mentioned a woman who had been praying for revival for years. But what she hadn't realized was her own need of revival. Convicted of the sin of bitterness toward another church member, she confessed her sin to that person and fellowship was once again restored.

A word of caution. Not all sin needs to be confessed publicly. Public confession of some sins would do more harm than good. The emphasis is on confessing to *one another* (the one you've harmed).

THE CHURCH SHOULD SEEK FOR THE BETTER GIFTS

"But earnestly desire the greater gifts" (1 Corinthians 12:31). "Pursue love, yet desire earnestly spiritual gifts, but especially that you may prophesy" (1 Corinthians 14:1). In each case the word *desire* is plural. Paul isn't telling individuals to desire specific gifts for themselves. They have already been distributed by the sovereign will of the Holy Spirit. (Paul does say, however, that the Corinthians were wrong to seek the gift of tongues. That was low on the totem pole. The better gift is prophecy.) They should seek after prophecy and other higher gifts.

It might be interesting to have someone in your congregation who can perform miracles, but Paul says that the ability to preach and teach is more important: " . . . second prophets, third teachers, *then* miracles" (1 Corinthians 12:28). It might be exciting to know someone with the gift of speaking a language who never studied it, but the gift of healing, helps, and administration is more valuable: " . . . *then* gifts of healing, helps, administration, various kinds of tongues" (1 Corinthians 12:28).

GIFTS ARE EFFECTIVE TO THE DEGREE THAT THEY ARE USED IN LOVE

Some people use their gifts exclusively for personal *entertainment* (i.e., gift of music) or personal *satisfaction* (i.e., gift of helps, working around the house). Some use their gifts primarily for *status* or acceptance (i.e., gift of preaching, teaching, counseling, administration, leadership). Some just like to be seen and admired by others (i.e., gift of music, giving, showing mercy, faith).

In 1 Corinthians 13:1–3 Paul outlines the gifts in four categories and concludes that the use of any of these gifts without love is meaningless.

A Public Gift (v. 1). "If I speak with the tongues of men and of angels, but do not have love, I have become a noisy gong or a clanging cymbal."

A Helpful Gift (v. 2a). "And if I have the gift of prophecy, and know all mysteries and all knowledge . . . but do not have love, I am nothing."

A Powerful Gift (v. 2b). "And if I have all faith, so as to remove mountains, but do not have love, I am nothing."

A Sacrificial Gift (v. 3). "And if I give all my possessions to feed the poor, and if I deliver my body to be burned, but do not have love, it profits me nothing."

Gifts of the Holy Spirit aren't an end in themselves. They are vehicles through which we express love to one another. Paul explains, "For you were called to freedom, brethren; only do not turn your freedom into an opportunity for the flesh, but *through love serve one another*" (Galatians 5:13).

CONGREGATIONS SHOULD SEEK GIFTS ACCORDING TO GOD'S PRIORITY SYSTEM

First on God's priority list is that the church pursues love (1 Corinthians 14:1). Jesus didn't say that "all men shall know that you are my disciples by your gifts." He said, "By this all men will know that you are my disciples, if you have love for one another" (John 13:35). God judges a church's discipleship on the basis of the members' love for each other, not on the number or quality of their gifts.

Many congregations pursue programs. Others pursue new members. Others pursue methods and organization. The Bible tells us to pursue love. And how better may a congregation exhibit this God-given love than by discovering, training, polishing, and using the gifts given them by God's Holy Spirit?

bibliography

Bennett, Dennis & Rita. *The Holy Spirit and You.* Plainfield, New Jersey: Logos International, 1971.

Bright, Bill. *How to Be Filled with the Spirit.* San Bernardino, Calif.: Campus Crusade for Christ, International, 1971.

Criswell, W. A. *The Holy Spirit in Today's World.* Grand Rapids, Michigan: Zondervan Publishing House, 1966.

Gangel, Kenneth O. *Leadership for Church Education.* Chicago: Moody, 1970.

Graham, Billy. *World Aflame.* Garden City, New York: Doubleday, 1965.

Gromacki, Robert G. *The Modern Tongues Movement.* Philadelphia: The Presbyterian & Reformed Publishing Company, 1967.

Grossmann, Siegfried. *There Are Other Gifts Than Tongues.* Wheaton, Ill.: Tyndale House Publishers, 1973.

Hendricks, Howard G. *Elijah: Confrontation, Conflict and Crisis.* Chicago: Moody Press, 1972.

Hendriksen, William. *New Testament Commentary: 1 & 2 Timothy & Titus.* Grand Rapids, Michigan: Baker Book House, 1957.

Johnson, Margaret. *18 and No Time to Waste.* Grand Rapids, Michigan: Zondervan Publishing House, 1971.

Kent, Homer. *The Pastoral Epistles.* Chicago: Moody Press, 1958.

Lindsey, Hal. *Satan Is Alive and Well on Planet Earth.* Grand Rapids, Mich.: Zondervan Publishing House, 1972.

LeTourneau, R. G. *Mover of Men and Mountains.* Chicago: Moody Press, 1972.

Neal, Emily Gardiner. *The Healing Power of Christ.* New York: Hawthorn, 1972.

Peter, Laurence J., and Hull, Raymond. *The Peter Principle.* New York: Bantam, 1970.

Ryrie, Charles C. *The Role of Women in the Church.* Chicago: Moody Press, 1968.

Roberts, Oral. *The Call.* Garden City, New York: Doubleday, 1972.

Sanders, J. Oswald. *The Holy Spirit and His Gifts.* Grand Rapids, Mich.: Zondervan Publishing House, 1970.

Schuller, Robert. *Move Ahead with Possibility Thinking.* Garden City, N.Y.: Doubleday & Co. Inc., 1967.

Stedman, Ray C. *Body Life.* Glendale, Calif.: Regal Books, 1972.

Tari, Mel, and Dudley, Cliff. *Like A Mighty Wind.* Carol Stream, Ill.: Creation House, 1971.

Torrey, Reuben A. *Divine Healing.* Grand Rapids, Mich.: Baker Book House, 1970.

Tournier, Paul. *Guilt and Grace.* New York: Harper & Row, 1962.

White, Ernest. *The Way of Release.* Fort Washington, Penna.: Christian Literature Crusade, 1960.